Collecting Social Media in Museums

Collecting Social Media in Museums draws attention to the importance of collecting social media as museum objects and explores the role of rapid response and born-digital collecting in documenting social history as it happens.

Drawing on a range of case studies and facilitated conversations with museum professionals and technology experts, the book discusses different approaches to incorporating creator content from social media into museum practice. It highlights the need to bridge the gap between traditional museum practices that focus only on material aspects and what the authors argue is increasingly fundamental to human experience and identity formation: Social media and digital cultural artefacts. Providing readers with the critical tools necessary for a rethinking of museum collecting practices in the digital age, the book highlights different projects that have navigated ethical, legal and copyright concerns for institutions. The book culminates with recommendations relating to the implementation of social media collecting strategies, ultimately calling for the museum to be more responsive to safeguarding the content that is generated online for future generations.

Collecting Social Media in Museums provides museum professionals around the world with valuable tools that will empower them to change their practices and respond to social media in real time, before it's too late to act. Scholars and students engaged in the study of museums, media and digital humanities will also find much to interest them within the pages of this book.

Craig Middleton is an Australian museum curator and creative producer whose research and practice centres on Lesbian, Gay, Bisexual, Transgender, Intersex, and Queer + (LGBTIQ+) people, communities and histories, while challenging traditional museological practices. Through his work, Craig champions digital engagement and collecting practices that prioritise the documentation of contemporary experience and that resonate with diverse communities.

Dr Caroline Wilson-Barnao is the Director of Museum Studies at the University of Queensland, where she teaches both theoretical and practical subjects. Her career spans two decades in communications and marketing in the cultural not-for-profit sector. Caroline writes on the digital transformation of cultural practice, which she explores in her book Digital Access and Museums as Platforms (2022). She is a member of the Digital Cultures and Society group and the Museums Association of Critical Heritage Studies, and is an accredited Higher Education Academy (HEA) Fellow.

Routledge Guides to Practice in Museums, Galleries and Heritage

This series provides essential practical guides for those working in museums, galleries and a variety of other heritage professions around the globe.

Including authored and edited volumes, the series will help to enhance practitioners' and students' professional knowledge and will also encourage the sharing of best practices between different countries, as well as between different types and sizes of organisations.

Titles published in the series include:

Institutional Change for Museums
A Practical Guide to Creating Polyvocal Spaces
Edited by Marianna Pegno and Kantara Souffrant

Ethics of Contemporary Collecting
Edited by Jen Kavanagh, Ellie Miles and Rosamund Lily West with Susanna Cordner

Cultivating Futures Thinking in Museums
Edited by Dr Kristin Alford

Leadership of Inclusive and Sustainable Cultural Organisations
A Practical Guide
Piotr Bienkowski and Hilary Mcgowan

Collecting Social Media in Museums
Craig Middleton and Caroline Wilson-Barnao

For more information about this series, please visit: https://www.routledge.com/Routledge-Guides-to-Practice-in-Museums-Galleries-and-Heritage/book-series/RGPMGH

Collecting Social Media in Museums

Craig Middleton and Caroline Wilson-Barnao

Routledge
Taylor & Francis Group
LONDON AND NEW YORK

Designed cover image: Getty Images

First published 2026
by Routledge
4 Park Square, Milton Park, Abingdon, Oxon OX14 4RN

and by Routledge
605 Third Avenue, New York, NY 10158

Routledge is an imprint of the Taylor & Francis Group, an informa business

British Library Cataloguing-in-Publication Data
A catalogue record for this book is available from the British Library

ISBN: 978-1-032-66964-9 (hbk)
ISBN: 978-1-032-60635-4 (pbk)
ISBN: 978-1-032-66965-6 (ebk)

DOI: 10.4324/9781032669656

Typeset in Times New Roman
by SPi Technologies India Pvt Ltd (Straive)

Contents

Acknowledgements

Many people have supported us through the creation of *Collecting Social Media in Museums*.

First and foremost, we want to thank those whom we interviewed, whose experiences, insights and ideas are inspiring to us and have enriched the content of this book: Suse Anderson, Foteini Aravani, Nic Carah, Seb Chan, Kirsty Cox, Bronwyn Dowdall, Dragan Espenschied, Kasja Hartig, Arran Rees, Jason Scott and Keir Winesmith.

Thank you to the institutions at which we work, the University of Queensland and the National Museum of Australia, for supporting us to undertake this project.

Over the course of almost two years that we worked on this project, we were joined at various times by students and emerging scholars who supported aspects of the research as part of internships, scholarships and as research assistants. These people provided great support, ideas and research that benefited this book: Eloise Cicero, Meg Herrmann, Kathleen Humphreys, Brittany Rissaman, Muhammad Fasha Rouf, Susan Sudbury, Chris Vernon and Zichen Zhang.

Thanks to Heidi Lowther, Chris Parry and Manas Roy at Routledge for their enthusiasm about, confidence in and support of our work, and to Susan Jarvis for her editorial prowess. We want to also thank the anonymous reviewers of our initial proposal, whose suggestions and advice helped us refine our ideas and move forward with confidence.

Last, but not least, we want to thank our loved ones: Craig's husband Malakai and Caroline's stepmother Robyn, and children Olive and Hunter, who supported us through the breakthroughs, the challenges and the long days, evenings and weekends spent writing.

1 Introduction

As we write this book, the Israel–Hamas war is ongoing, since Hamas-led militant groups attacked Israeli civilian communities and military bases on 7 October 2023 (Centre for Preventative Action, 2025). Subsequently, the death toll has escalated, millions have been displaced and the destruction has continued unabated, resulting in a humanitarian crisis that has attracted global attention (UNRWA, 2025). For those not in conflict zones, the realities of war are something that were once only understood through newspapers, radio, photography and television; today, however, social media plays a unique role in representing conflicts. Palestinian citizens have turned into content creators to share their experiences of life in Gaza during the conflict. Bashar Alzaanin (@basharzaanin), a Gazan bodybuilder, used his social media feed to discuss his connection with his homeland and to communicate the impact of the war on his life. On 2 May 2024, he posted a video from his life before the war, working out at one of Gaza's largest facilities, Oxygen Gym, prior to his displacement. The video is accompanied by the words 'after' and 'before' (Alzaanin, 2024) and ends with the footage of Alzaanin's friend and bodybuilding coach, Maher, lifting weights in the ruins of the once-busy fitness centre. The caption reads: 'As you can see the occupation destroyed everything, every place, every moment, every memory' (Alzaanin, 2024). Mohamed Al Khalidi (@m7md_vo) similarly shared content from life in a war zone with a social video titled 'Wedding in war?!' (Al Khalidi, 2024), comprising an edited selection of smartphone videos from a wedding in Gaza on 28 May. The caption reads: 'Imagine yourself getting married in a war and in a tent! We really love life' (Al Khalidi, 2024). Palestinian journalist Rama Zaanoun (r.z.gaza) documented the atrocities of war on her feed. On 30 May 2024, she posted a video of a young boy screaming and crying. The accompanying caption explained, 'He stands in front of their tent, watching his father being burned alive, saying "My father is gone, and I want to be with him". No child should wish to be burned alive. The pain and trauma are unimaginable' (Zaanoun, 2024). The first example shows the physical destruction of war, which many of us might consume through mainstream media, textbooks and history lessons. The second shows that celebrations of everyday life carry on even in the most unimaginable contexts, speaking to our humanity and relationships. The third reveals the horrors of war – fear, loss,

DOI: 10.4324/9781032669656-1

death – and reveals insights into the perpetrators of such atrocities. These accounts of war are unfiltered. They are not framed within a 'news' context or presented to an audience through high-quality, edited footage. These posts and the stories they tell are perhaps more human – they offer us a unique insight, not only into the conflict but also into the experiences of everyday people who live and die through it.

These are only three examples of thousands of Palestinians using social media to document and share their experiences of war with the world. While most mainstream media focus their attention on attacks, the realities of everyday life in a war zone are now communicated by citizen-creators on social media. A Toronto-based filmmaker, Kanwal Ahmed, reflects on their experience of the war as a social media user.

> Everyone is getting a chance to tell their own stories … People can tell for themselves … And it's very hard to look away when you're seeing somebody sitting in a pile of rubble, or if you're seeing a five-year-old girl crying next to her father's dead body.
>
> (Kaur, 2024)

This is not unlike the impact television had on communicating the Vietnam War, when everyday citizens were, for the first time, exposed to visions of warplanes dropping bombs and service people in combat (Mandelbaum, 1982, p. 157). In contrast to the Vietnam War, when television stories shared graphic content that influenced public perception of conflicts, social media goes further, not only creating records of conflict zones but also of sites of everyday experience. It offers the viewer an insight into the lived realities of everyday people – just like them. The content being produced by creators such as those in Gaza is important. They not only share the atrocities of war; they create a record of human experience. The examples provided here demonstrate how social media platforms in the twenty-first century are being used to connect people and ideas across time and space, to seek support, to deploy activism and advocacy, and to draw attention to lived realities. This becomes even more important when we consider the ban on international reporters and journalists entering Gaza (Sherwood, 2023) and the reality that social media accounts will act as important records of independent observations of the conflict. Social media in this context provides more than a communication tool; it is where creators – people just like us – are producing a large and important record of human history, and museums as institutions tasked with collecting and preserving objects of historical significance must pay closer attention to this.

Cultural heritage in a digital world

Within a global context, where humans are reliant on digital technologies and practices to live their lives, this book considers what social media means to human history – that is, what it can tell us about our culture, memories, collective values and norms. We consider why we need to preserve it for future generations, and we articulate the role of museums in doing so. We contend that social media plays an important role in generating more inclusive and representative histories through its function as a community-building technology in spaces that foster the everyday expressions of human empathy and connection (Dobson et al., 2018; Hjorth, 2018; McGlotten, 2014). The content or outputs of such technologies – objects, if you will – capture embodied memories and experiences; the posts and comments create meaning that holds contemporary and historical value. From sharing a recipe on TikTok or posting baby pictures on Instagram to promoting an event on Facebook and creating connections and relationships on Grindr and Bumble, our material practices are deeply entwined with the digital realm. When we really think about this, most of us can identify parts of our lives that are facilitated through screens and internet technologies. Yet, despite this obvious reality, where people and screens are meaningfully connected, museums continue to use social media primarily for audience engagement and marketing purposes. This can involve other – sometimes participatory – activities, but it generally encompasses the institution posting public relations and marketing content on social media. We are not suggesting that these uses are not important, and we applaud the excellent work of museums in harnessing the power of social media for meaningful audience engagement.

In general, there is a lack of acknowledgement of the cultural significance of social media that recognises its value in being collected by museums, despite the work of some dedicated individuals and groups (Museum Social Media Cultures Research Network, 2025). Without doubt, the question of how to collect social media is tricky. Unsurprisingly, not many cultural institutions collect it at all, and those that do face serious challenges regarding the digital infrastructures and financial commitments required to acquire and care for it in the long term (Nikolaou, 2024, p. 1787). Attempts to collect social media are complicated further by the varying missions and policy documents of collecting institutions, many of which were developed at a time when born-digital materials were less common or non-existent. Despite these obstacles, this book argues that there is a palpable need for museums to collect social media as museum objects or risk losing important experiences, moments and collective memories. In fact, we have undoubtedly lost so much already as social media companies establish and collapse, and platforms go in and out of fashion.

In this book, we do not claim to be technical experts, for there are scholars and practitioners engaging with the technical challenges of collecting born-digital objects in museums, including digital preservation (Digital Preservation Coalition, 2025; ICOM International Committee for Documentation, 2025; Museum and Social Media Cultures Research Network, 2025). Instead, we offer a perspective that goes hand in hand with the technical, articulating a curatorial approach to collecting social media in museums. Acknowledging that Instagram, Facebook, TikTok, WeChat and many more social media that will come and go are primary custodians of contemporary digital culture, we contend that their outputs can, and should, be understood as objects worthy of cultural collections. Currently, these social media objects are not regulated or archived in ways that are publicly accessible – unlike, for example, the output of newspapers and broadcast media, much of which is collected by libraries and archives.

Libraries and archives have long been at the forefront of digital preservation; however, these institutions are repositories that do not necessarily play an interpretive role in presenting the content they house to audiences in the same way museums do. Their approaches differ from those taken by museums. In general, libraries and archives collect more comprehensively. For example, libraries will collect published material (analogue and digital) from a specific jurisdiction (a country or a locality) and might endeavour to represent all published material from that region – for example, the National Library of Australia's collection strategy outlines that the institution has 'an ongoing role to comprehensively collect and preserve Australian documentary heritage' (National Library of Australia, 2025). Archives too – especially government archives – might be required to collect and retain certain official records comprehensively for the long-term benefit of a country, region or organisation (National Archives of Australia, 2025). Museums, on the other hand, collect based on certain criteria of significance – aesthetic, cultural, social, political and so on – informed by their focus or theme. They are tasked to present objects collected to the public, often through interpretive practices and informed by a curatorial rationale – for example, the National Museum of Australia's Collections Development Policy states that 'the Museum's collecting is necessarily selective and representative, rather than comprehensive' (National Museum of Australia, 2025). While it is not the role of museums to collect everything related to their focus or theme, they have a responsibility to collect objects that are significant to human history and that can be used to tell both the personal and collective stories of a group of people. Within this landscape of collecting institutions, this book argues that social media must be considered as significant to history and that museums have a unique role in collecting social media objects – not comprehensively, like other collecting institutions, but selectively in order to preserve human interactions with social media to ensure its impact and influence are recorded for posterity. So, how might museums best identify and collect? and what practices, tools, policies and infrastructures are required to do this work? To answer these questions, we unpack the implications for museums as they shift their practices to collect social media.

In the late twentieth century, a reconsideration of traditional methods of museum collection and display began to take place, influenced by calls for democratisation (Hooper-Greenhill, 1992) and the principles of 'new museology' (Vergo, 1989). Scholars such as Graham Black (2012) and Nina Simon (2016) evidence the call for museums to continue this transformation if they are to remain relevant. We argue that this transformation includes the acknowledgement that social media is culturally significant and worthy of collecting and that museums (as opposed to other collecting institutions) have a unique role to play in addressing this. We also acknowledge that social media platforms operate according to completely different logics than museums in terms of how content is engaged with and displayed. This makes the task of understanding and collecting social media a challenge for museums; however, there is much to learn from the logic of social media that can shift this mindset. Chiara Zuanni refers to social media platforms as assemblages that consist of 'files, servers, databases, code ... whose agency is established through a seamless flow of information between these components and the human actors around them - shaping their content, contexts, and infrastructure' (2021, p. 190). For instance, TikTok's algorithm selects the videos that will appear in a user's feed, ensuring that each individual's 'for you' page is highly personalised. The algorithm changes and adjusts what users see in real time, informed by a user's viewing history, preferences, favourites, comments, likes and so on. The content being produced by a user also informs algorithmic decisions. Individual users apply different effects, music, hashtags and so forth to their content to attract attention from other users. All the while, the algorithm collects information about how users interact with each other, further informing which accounts' content is being sourced from and which content is being sent to unique feeds. The content shared on the platform is transient, disappearing 24 hours after it is posted. Despite content disappearing from users' feeds, the platform scrapes information from the content, such as geolocation, device and app setting information, which is relayed to its servers and presumably stored in cloud-based data centres (Degrippo, 2020). Within this context, the functionalities of the algorithm and the environment in which the content is housed change over time.

In contrast, museums have developed their own organising principles and classification systems (ICOM, 2017). Objects are identified, researched and collected on the basis of their significance to a group of people, a place or an event. Once collected, objects are meticulously documented and relocated to storage facilities, where they are permanently housed for long-term preservation. Collection-management systems are populated with data relating to an object, its materiality, condition, significance and provenance, among other things. The data stored in the collection-management systems are agreed to and informed by industry and organisational standards. While best practice changes over time, the fundamental logic of how museums collect remains largely unchanged. It is ultimately unlikely that museums will have the ability to impact the logics and practices of corporate social media agencies, so it will be necessary for museums to adapt their own logics and practices to make room for the collecting of social media, especially if they are to understand such content, as this book articulates, as culturally and historically significant.

At this point, you may be asking what exactly makes social media content so different from other object types and whether museums really need to alter their practices to collect it. Creating social media content is now an everyday practice for many people in the twenty-first century. Of course, not all the content and data shared on social media should be considered as objects of cultural significance from a museum's perspective, nor are they collectable. Instead, like all objects, social media objects are required to fit into a museum's existing collection frameworks and policies, and must align with the criteria set by the museum if they are to transform from being content to objects. What constitutes a social media object then depends on the context surrounding it – who is producing it, who is collecting it, why it is important, where it is being shared online and what it can tell us about a particular social, cultural, scientific or artistic moment, phenomenon or practice. Social media objects are, therefore, similar to other museum objects in that they are expected to offer an insight into human experience. Social media objects, however, ask more of museums when assessing their significance. The online environments, comments, likes, shares and reactions all become a focus of significance assessments. Sarah Higgins explains that simple digital objects are 'discrete digital items; such as textual files, images or sound files, along with their related identifiers and metadata' (2008, p. 137) and that complex digital objects are 'discrete digital objects, made by combining a number of other digital objects' (2008, p. 137). Social media objects, for example, could include text, photos and videos, but also user engagement in the form of likes, comments and shares, and exist in algorithmic contexts that impact their own histories. In this way, social media objects are complex digital objects that require their own considerations when it comes to their collecting by museums. In the chapters that follow, the case studies presented and the core principles articulated in the conclusion will support museum professionals and others to undertake the work of collecting social media in museums.

Acknowledging the work of others

To understand the context in which emerging collecting practices develop and change, we must first consider the pioneering work and scholarship produced to date. It is within this scholarly and practical context that this book exists, bringing together the ideas and perspectives of others in conversation with our own in one place. Much of the literature on social media and museums discusses how to use it to attract audiences or enhance visitor experiences and meaning-making (Drotner & Christian Schrøder, 2013; Kelly, 2013; Russo et al., 2008). In museums, social media is commonly understood as a way to connect with online audiences, market upcoming exhibitions and programmes, seek audience feedback and maintain an understanding of current trends that might influence museum outputs, all of which stem from its use for promotional purposes. Very little has been written about understanding it as cultural heritage, and even less about why or how to collect it. The scholarly literature consists largely of edited collections and individual peer-reviewed papers that provide highly specific accounts of collecting (Fahy, 2005; Knell, 2017; Miller, 2020). Surprisingly, very few works exist that grapple with contemporary collecting in general or focus on how museums approach social media within the context of contemporary collecting. Some of the most prominent works include Kevin Moist and David Banash's (2013) edited collection, *Contemporary Collecting: Objects, Practices, and the Fate of Things*, which includes important discussions about different forms of digital collecting. Owain Rhys's (2011) book *Contemporary Collecting: Theory and Practice* also offers a significant contribution to exploring how museums might shift their practices to accommodate new approaches to collecting using a variety of case studies. However, it does not include a dedicated focus on born-digital objects or on social media. Kylie Message's (2020) book *Collecting Activism, Archiving Occupy Wall Street* considers how rapid-response collecting can be used to help formulate a more responsive institution, particularly during periods of social upheaval, but does not connect these findings explicitly to social media. Likewise, Kirsten Drotner and Kim Christian Schrøder's (2013) edited collection *Museum Communication and Social Media: The Connected Museum* explores the range of ways by which a museum might integrate social media into its engagement and collecting practice, drawing on case studies. However, this publication does not focus on how to collect social media objects. Keir Winesmith and Suse Anderson's (2020) *The Digital Future of Museums: Conversations and Provocations* also considers the transformation of the museum as a result of digital shifts, but does not focus specifically on social media collecting. These authors and their work are extremely important, and we can learn much from their ideas, perspectives and case studies, which inform a context in which social media collecting exists.

One of the most significant publications focused on social media collecting in museums is Arran Rees's (2021) PhD thesis, 'Remixing Museology: An Approach to Collecting Social Media in Museums,' which presents an autoethnographic account of his work as a collections manager, along with interviews with practitioners. Drawing on Lessig's notion of 'remix,' Rees demonstrates that internet users reappropriate meaning into memes, which in turn unsettles how museums have traditionally understood how they go about collecting objects. Rees (2021, p. 200) argues that we have moved from a 'Read Only culture' to a 'Read Write culture,' where 'we read, edit, and re-appropriate cultural content and create something new.' Rees (p. 213) goes on to suggest that museums need to regard these 'Read, Write culture' outputs as challenging the existing collecting practices of museums, which are orientated towards collecting material objects. He stresses the need to adopt better acquisition processes that address issues of 'provenance, copyright and ownership' (p. 213). He argues that for museums to be in a position to collect social media, they need to approach collections-management processes with a different mindset that is better equipped to respond to new and emerging object types, including memes. Rees' contribution is especially helpful as it makes it possible to understand a social media object as owned by multiple users. Rees points out that museums cannot approach this form of collecting following existing processes for physical or analogue material culture.

This finding echoes Asti Sherring (2023), who, in her research with conservators, demonstrates the need to draw upon their own personal frameworks when making decisions about contemporary objects. These 'values and ethical considerations' of individual conservators can shape the extent of an 'intervention, the choice of materials and techniques, the desired outcome of the conservation treatment and the potential broader effects on society and creator communities' (Sherring, 2023, p. 2). Similarly, Heather MacNeil (2004) draws attention to the different but connected contexts in which social media communication takes place, making it more difficult to ascertain origin and ownership. In participatory culture, social media objects have multiple authors, which can make it difficult to determine who created social media content or determine its origin. A recurrent theme in the literature is the need for curators, conservators and other specialist museum staff involved in the process of collecting, cataloguing and displaying contemporary social media objects to be adaptable. In fact, it is not always possible for museums to own social media objects in the same way that they might own a physical artefact, so they may need to adopt a licensing policy that is similar to that of media platforms (Rees, 2021). This potentially involves the museums collecting social media content in a shared ownership framework between the creator and the museum.

Another book that offers a dedicated focus on social media collecting is Boogh et al.'s (2020) *Connect to Collect: Approaches to Collecting Social Digital Photography in Museums and Archives*. This publication is significant because it provides direct advice on how museums might go about collecting social media by drawing on relevant literature and case studies. Importantly, it presents a web application that can be used by museums for collecting social media and involves users actively uploading photos and metadata. Drawing on Nathan Jurgenson's (2019, p. 12) use of the term 'social digital photography' to refer to the production of imagery on social media as a cultural practice that extends beyond a 'specific photo or even any specific social media platform,' the book demonstrates how social media is used to convey information and stories. Concluding with recommendations about policy and practice, and offering suggestions about the role of museums and how their infrastructures can be adapted to this type of collecting, Boogh et al.'s book is one of the most significant contributions to the field published to date.

Our intention is that this book will contribute to the emerging body of scholarship and practice through articulating curatorially informed approaches to collecting social media. By centring the curatorial practice of significance against a backdrop of contemporary and rapid-response collecting, collection management and conservation – which is well articulated in the emerging literature – we hope that the book becomes a companion to the technical contributions associated with collecting social media in museums.

Motivations, scope, limits and approach

Given our backgrounds as a museum curator (Craig) and a communications and museum studies scholar (Caroline), we share an interest in the digital practices of museums. This ranges from communications to display and interpretation, all the way through the museum's collecting practices. Caroline's first book, *Digital Access and Museums and Platforms* (2022), for example, explored how cultural collections are made available using digital technologies. We met online at a Museum Next Digital Collections Summit in 2021 when Craig was presenting on the National Museum of Australia's project *Momentous* – a digital project seeking to document social media and digital cultural output in response to the 2019–2020 Australian bushfires and the COVID-19 pandemic, which we discuss more in Chapter 4. We started a conversation about *Momentous* and the role of museums in collecting social media more generally. This led to us co-authoring a paper, 'Redefining Crisis in Museums: Insiders' Perspectives on Digital Engagement,' with our colleague Lisa Enright (Wilson-Barnao et al., 2023) about *Momentous* and how the project fitted into the landscape of digital collecting. Over the course of four years, we have had innumerable conversations that led us to identify a need for this book. Our professional relationship began online, and we have written this book together in two different Australian cities using internet-based digital technologies to do so. For us, the digital realm has led to the creation of this scholarly output, which further asserts the importance of capturing how the internet and its many subcultures have impacted people's lives and cultural production, as they have ours.

Our motivations for writing this book were many and varied but stemmed from a dissatisfaction that, despite public internet cultures – including social media – having been around since the mid-1990s, museums have not made substantial progress in understanding social media as historically significant and, despite the best efforts of many professionals, continue to de-prioritise the work over other more traditional modes of collecting. From this perspective, the technological and/or resourcing challenges of collecting digital-born material tend to take priority over assessing historical significance. This is not to suggest that technological or resourcing challenges are unimportant or that, without the appropriate infrastructure, a museum should collect social media or other digital material. It is rather that determining the significance or importance of the material should come first, and that grappling with technological and/or resourcing challenges is a secondary consideration that may well lead to collecting or not collecting. However, it is our aim to endeavour to shift the narrative so that the significance of social media is considered just as important as the significance of physical objects. Museums, then, might give themselves permission to experiment with and potentially overcome some of the more complex challenges of technically collecting social media.

In what follows, we consider social media as significant to human history and the critical role that everyday device users play in documenting social history as it unfolds online. We unpack the practices of museums in assessing the significance of such material and draw on several case studies detailing the kinds of projects that museums are undertaking to collect social media. We also delve into the ethical challenges faced by museums, and that they are required to attend to, when collecting social media – not to halt progress, but to acknowledge a volatile and changing space within which social media exists.

We know the word 'museum' means different things to different people and has a variety of meanings in different cultural contexts. The new International Council of Museums (ICOM) definition of museums in the twenty-first century, adopted at an Extraordinary General Assembly of ICOM in Prague on 24 August 2022, states that:

> A museum is a not-for-profit, permanent institution in the service of society that researches, collects, conserves, interprets and exhibits tangible and intangible heritage. Open to the public, accessible and inclusive, museums foster diversity and sustainability. They operate and communicate ethically, professionally and with the participation of communities, offering varied experiences for education, enjoyment, reflection and knowledge sharing.
>
> (ICOM, 2022)

It is within the context of this definition that this book exists. We contend that social media is a form of intangible cultural heritage, and as such, fits firmly within the remit of museums as described by ICOM. Furthermore, while applicable to many kinds of museums, this book is framed within a context of social and cultural histories. This framing is important to understand the importance of social media to human history. While we believe the contribution of this book is applicable in other contexts – art, science and natural history – our focus is very much on museums of social and cultural histories, which preserve objects of people and societies, and collect the personal stories of everyday people.

What this book does not address in detail are the technological aspects of collecting social media. As already noted, there are many professionals, conservators, digital preservationists and other technologists who are engaging with the work of how exactly to capture, record and collect digital cultural material in ways that support long-term preservation, access and use. We acknowledge this work as extremely important and encourage readers to use this book and what it offers in conversation with other scholarship and practice documents that speak directly to technological approaches to collecting digital-born objects. Our contribution to the scholarship provides something complementary and, at the same time, asserts the importance of the non-technical curatorial work required to move forward the overall project of collecting social media in museums.

Within this overarching context, this book aims to address four key research questions:

1 Is social media of value to museums?
2 How does social media trouble current museum practices?
3 How can museums approach collecting social media?
4 What are the ethical considerations museums must engage with in order to collect social media?

These broad research questions inform each main chapter of the book.

Organisation of the book

Collecting Social Media in Museums is organised into six chapters that are framed by this introduction (Chapter 1) and a conclusion (Chapter 6) that outlines key principles for collecting social media in museums. The remaining chapters are divided by their unique focus: content as object, significance, collecting and ethics. At the end of each chapter, you will encounter summaries of interviews with professionals and academics whose work is engaged with social media. They offer varied perspectives and ideas on collecting social media in museums. In total, we draw on 10 semi-structured interviews with professionals based both within Australia and overseas. These interviews were too valuable to bury within the footnotes of the book, so we have presented them in conversation with the book's main arguments, and we hope you find value in this approach.

Chapter 2 argues that social media is culturally significant in an age where humans rely on digital technologies to live their lives and express their identities. Presenting examples of content housed on social media platforms, we highlight the different kinds of social media currently being created and the types of content that museums might collect. We characterise museum creators as capturing important social, political and historical events – providing the museum with multiple voices and perspectives, and reinforcing the need for museums to engage and collect in these spaces.

Chapter 3 acknowledges that museums cannot collect everything in the age of information. This chapter begins by outlining contemporary, rapid-response and born-digital collecting as frameworks within which collecting social media exists. We draw on the museological concept of significance to explore how the historic, aesthetic, scientific and social values of social media objects are determined. Exploring the benefits and limitations of significance criteria, we highlight the challenges in identifying the significance of social media content in contrast to physical objects. Using social media not yet collected by museums, we develop case studies to consider the practice of significance and unpack new questions and considerations asked of museums when assessing the significance of social media.

Chapter 4 provides an overview of some of the different approaches that museums, libraries, archives and other entities have taken to collecting social media internationally. In doing so, we have identified and articulated a range of projects, framing them within six approaches to collecting social media: Automated social media archiving; donated content and data; collecting without collecting; collecting directly from social media; third-party-initiated collecting; and simulation to support museums to understand which approaches might work in their unique contexts and within their resourcing and technological parameters. We provide an analysis of the benefits and drawbacks of each approach to collecting social media, acknowledging the need to experiment and review in a rapidly changing space.

Chapter 5 investigates some of the more complex issues faced by museums when collecting social media: Platforms, storage and sustainability; privacy and protection, including the Right to be Forgotten; commercialisation and corporate players; and synthetic media, including artificial intelligence. To do this, we have drawn on scholarly literature and social media policy documents from major platforms such as Facebook, Instagram and TikTok to extract, explore and generalise current and emerging ethical issues in the space of collecting social media in museums.

In Chapter 6, we conclude the book by articulating six core principles, informed by what we have learnt, that we believe can guide museum professionals as they undertake to collect social media in museums. They are:

1 acknowledge the importance of digital cultural heritage
2 don't collect everything, be intentional rather than comprehensive
3 don't wait, engage now and be adaptable
4 experiment frequently and widely
5 seek consent, but within a risk-positive approach
6 embrace change and redefine control

These core principles consolidate the ideas, challenges, opportunities and considerations that we have learnt from our research, but are not a blueprint or guidebook on the practicalities of collecting social media. Our intention is that the core principles will be used to ground arguments and business cases for collecting social media in museums. This includes when arguing for technological and infrastructure support to do the work; to support practitioners from a curatorial standpoint; and to support museums to confidently move forward to undertake the challenging work of collecting social media.

Ultimately, *Collecting Social Media in Museums* aims to open up a conversation about museums actively engaging with the digital realm, its significance to human experience and history, the many and varied approaches taken to collecting it and the new questions museums need to ask of their collections and their practices in order to do it. This book seeks to bridge the gap between historic museum practices that focus on the physical, tangible and material aspects of collections and social media, and the born-digital objects that comprise them, which we argue are meaningful human experiences worthy of collection.

References

Al Khalidi, M. [@m7md_vo]. (2024). Imagine yourself getting married in a war and in a tent! Instagram. Accessed 16 February 2025 from www.instagram.com/m7md_vo/reel/C7cE3rrtkgp

Alzaanin, B. [@basharzaanin]. (2024). This is the greatest and biggest GYM in gaza @oxygengymgaza. Instagram. Accessed 16 February 2025 from https://www.instagram.com/p/C7rbcmJNk8R

Black, G. (2012). *Transforming museums in the 21st century*. Routledge.

Boogh, E., Hartig, K., Jensen, B., Uimonen, P., & Wallenius, A. (Eds.). (2020). *Connect to collect: Approaches to collecting social digital photography in museums and archives*. Stitelsen Nordiska museet. Accessed 27 January 2023 from www.academia.edu/43046542/Connect_to_Collect_Approaches_to_Collecting_Social_Digital_Photography_in_Museums_and_Archives

Centre for Preventative Action. (2025). Israeli–Palestinian conflict. Accessed 18 May 2025 from www.cfr.org/global-conflict-tracker/conflict/israeli-palestinian-conflict

Degrippo, S. (2020). Understanding the information TikTok gathers and stores. proofpoint. Accessed 27 January 2023 from www.proofpoint.com/us/blog/threat-protection/understanding-information-tiktok-gathers-and-stores

Digital Preservation Coalition. (2025). Website. Accessed 18 May 2025 from www.dpconline.org

Dobson, A. S., Carah, N., & Robards, B. (2018). Digital intimate publics and social media: Towards theorising public lives on private platforms. In A. S. Dobson, B. Robards, & N. Carah (Eds.), *Digital intimate publics and social media* (pp. 3–27). Palgrave Macmillan.

Drotner, K., & Christian Schrøder, K. (2013). *Museum communication and social Media: The connected museum*. Routledge.

Fahy, A. (2005). *Collections management*. Routledge.

Higgins, S. (2008). The DCC curation lifecycle model. *The International Journal of Digital Curation*, *3*(1), 134–140. https://doi.org/10.2218/ijdc.v3i1.48

Hjorth, L. (2018). Snapshots of afterlife: The cultural intimacies of posthumous camera phone practices. In A. S. Dobson, B. Robards, & N. Carah (Eds.), *Digital intimate publics and social media*. Palgrave Macmillan. https://doi.org/10.1007/978-3-319-97607-5_4

Hooper-Greenhill, E. (1992). *Museums and the shaping of knowledge*. Routledge. https://doi.org/10.4324/9780203415825

ICOM. (2017). *ICOM code of ethics for museums*. International Council of Museums. Accessed 18 May 2025 from https://icom.museum/en/resources/standards-guidelines/code-of-ethics/

ICOM. (2022). *Museum definition*. International Council of Museums. Accessed 16 February 2025 from https://icom.museum/en/resources/standards-guidelines/museum-definition/

ICOM International Committee for Documentation. (2025). Website. Accessed 18 May 2025 from https://cidoc.mini.icom.museum

Jurgenson, N. (2019). *The social photo: On photography and social media*. Verso.

Kaur, H. (2024, 19 January). *Palestinians are documenting the war for millions on social media. Their followers have come to see them as family*. CNN. Accessed 2 June 2024 from https://edition.cnn.com/2024/01/19/world/palestinians-x-tiktok-instagram-gaza-cec/index.html

Kelly, L. (2013). The connected museum in the world of social media. In K. Drotner, & K. Christian Schrøder (Eds.), *Museum communication and social media: The connected museum* (pp. 54–71). Routledge.

Knell, S. (2017). *Museums and the future of collecting*. Routledge.

MacNeil, H. (2004). Contemporary archival diplomatics as a method of inquiry: Lessons learned from two research projects. *Archival Science*, *4*, 199–232. https://doi.org/10.1007/s10502-005-2592-x

Mandelbaum, M. (1982). Vietnam: The television war. *Daedalus*, *111*(4), 157–169. http://www.jstor.org/stable/20024822

McGlotten, S. (2014). *Virtual intimacies: Media, affect, and queer sociality*. State University of New York Press.

Message, K. (2020). *Collecting activism, archiving occupy wall street*. Routledge.

Miller, S. (2020). *Museum collection ethics: Acquisition, stewardship, and interpretation*. Rowman & Littlefield.

Moist, K., & Banash, D. (Eds.). (2013). *Contemporary collecting: Objects, practices, and the fate of things*. Scarecrow Press.

Museum Social Media Cultures Research Network. (2025). Website. Accessed 18 May 2025 from www.museumsocialmedia.com

National Archives of Australia. (2025). What we do. Accessed 18 May 2025 from www.naa.gov.au/about-us/what-we-do

National Library of Australia. (2025). Collecting strategy. Accessed 18 May 2025 from www.library.gov.au/visit/about-us/corporate-information/corporate-strategies/collecting-strategy

National Museum of Australia. (2025). Collections development policy. Accessed 18 May 2025 from www.nma.gov.au/about/corporate/policies/collections-development

Nikolaou, P. (2024). Museums and the post-digital: Revisiting challenges in the digital transformation of museums. *Heritage*, *7*, 1784–1800. https://doi.org/10.3390/heritage7030084

Rees. A. (2021). Remixing museology: An approach to collecting social media in museums. PhD Thesis, University of Leeds. Accessed 16 February 2025 from https://etheses.whiterose.ac.uk/id/eprint/29542/1/ArranJRees_Remixing-Museology_Thesis-Final.pdf

Rhys, O. (2011). *Contemporary collecting: Theory and practice*. MuseumsEtc.

Russo, A., Watkins, J., Kelly, L., & Chan, S. (2008). Participatory communication with social media. *Curator: The Museum Journal*, *51*(1), 21–31. https://doi.org/10.1111/j.2151-6952.2008.tb00292.x

Sherring, A. (2023). Embracing humanness in cultural materials conservation: A roundtable discussion with conservation professionals on ethics, values and the future. *AICCM Bulletin*, *44*(1–2), 6–18. https://doi.org/10.1080/10344233.2024.2312755

Sherwood, H. (2023, 12 December). 'Hugely frustrating': International media seek to overcome Gaza ban. *The Guardian*. Accessed 2 June 2025 from www.theguardian.com/world/2023/dec/12/hugely-frustrating-international-media-seek-to-overcome-gaza-ban

Simon, N. (2016). *The art of relevance*. Museum 2.0.

United Nations Relief and Works Agency (UNRWA). 2025. *UNRWA situation report #165 on the humanitarian crisis in the Gaza Strip and the West Bank, including East Jerusalem*. Accessed 2 June 2025 from www.unrwa.org/resources/reports/unrwa-situation-report-165-situation-gaza-strip-and-west-bank-including-east-jerusalem#:~:text=According%

Vergo, P. (1989). *The new museology*. Reaktion Books.

Wilson-Barnao, C. (2022). *Digital access and museums as platforms*. Routledge.

Wilson-Barnao, C., Middleton, C., & Enright. L. (2023). Redefining crisis in museums: Insiders' perspectives on digital engagement. *Curator: The Museum Journal*, *66*(2), 351–365. https://doi.org/10.1111/cura.12546

Winesmith, K., & Anderson. S. (2020). *The digital future of museums: Conversations and provocations*. Routledge.

Zaanoun, R. [r.z.gaza]. (2024). He stands in front of their tent, watching his father being burned alive. *Threads*. Accessed 16 February 2025 from www.threads.net/@r.z.gaza/post/C7jP8wcC0Nq?xmt=AQGzM2lFOMmHaJPGkFL72p4jNV6qpUsTpX5npswACPpD7w

Zuanni, C. (2021). Theorizing born digital objects: Museums and contemporary materialities. *Museum & Society*, *19*(2), 184–198. https://doi.org/10.29311/mas.v19i2.3790

2 Social media content as object

I (Craig) am a millennial. I was born in 1988. The following year, Australia made its first internet connection through the University of Melbourne, and by the mid-1990s, everyday Australians were gaining access to and participating in the public internet. I don't really remember these major socio-economic milestones happening: I was too young to be watching the news. However, what it meant for my childhood was growing up in a fast-paced and changing technological landscape that influenced how I experienced my life as a young person. I am probably part of the last generation of people to have experienced unplugging the landline telephone and plugging the ethernet cable into the wall, then waiting an agonising two to three minutes as the home internet connected, at the same time disabling my childhood home's ability to make and receive phone calls, much to my parents' never-ending frustration. The internet meant that instead of sitting on the phone for hours with my school friends, I would use chat applications online to connect with them, sharing our experiences of the day, gossiping and dreaming about the future. One such application was MSN Messenger – a staple for a millennial of my age. This application was the reason why I set up my first email address, composed of a combination of silly words (not to be repeated here) that stayed with me until I reached employment age, when I realised just how childish it really was. MSN Messenger allowed me to connect more deeply with my school friends, keep in touch with people who moved schools and cities, and create space for me to make new friends outside of the specific group of people I happened to be at school with – these people were often added into a chat conversation by people I already knew, an excellent feature of the application. For a queer person living in suburban South Australia in the 1990s and early 2000s, the internet and its many applications played an important role in my own identity formation. I was able to access websites that shared experiences of gay men that I simply didn't see or have access to in my everyday life. It allowed me to explore different ways of being in the world, at least then, not offered to me as a path I might follow in my own life. MSN Messenger is a key site of my queer story, and it became a site of a key milestone in my life. I was 17 years old, in my final year of high school. I remember sitting on my single bed with what now seems like an awfully chunky laptop. I logged on to MSN Messenger, which I did most

DOI: 10.4324/9781032669656-2

nights, and I drafted a message: 'I need to tell you something.' I sent this message to a close friend with whom, because of MSN Messenger, I had built a strong and trusting relationship. She wrote back, 'Of course, anything.' I typed, deleted, redrafted and typed again. It felt like the longest two minutes of my life as I finally typed what I needed to say and anxiously clicked the send button. My chest was so tight, and I was short of breath as I stared at what I just sent, waiting for a reply: 'I am gay.' I came out on MSN Messenger. I no longer have access to my messaging history on the application; however, MSN Messenger is inextricably linked to my identity as a queer person today. If I had my time again, and I knew what I do now, I might have documented that interaction in some way and kept it as evidence of a foundational moment in my life. It is moments like mine – moments of real human experience, of life – that happen on social media every day, every minute, every second, yet are not (always) being kept by the individuals, the platforms or memory institutions such as museums.

Museums and social media

Communication scholars Caleb Carr and Rebecca Hayes acknowledge that there is no agreed-upon definition of social media and instead offer the following:

> Social media are Internet-based channels that allow users to opportunistically interact and selectively self-present, either in real-time or asynchronously, with both broad and narrow audiences who derive value from user-generated content and the perception of interaction with others.
> (2015, p. 50)

This definition is necessarily complex. For us, it identifies key aspects of social media that acknowledge its human – and not just technological – aspects. The first is 'interact,' suggesting that the media is necessarily social and requires people to connect with others through its use. The second is 'self-present,' which signals social media's role in identity and identity formation. The third is 'audiences,' which identifies social media as a site of gathering and as networked and relational. Finally, 'user-generated content' places people at the centre of what is created, posted, liked, commented on and shared on social media. Furthermore, we argue that social media should be understood as always entwined with the material world – recognising that it is produced by creators (human beings), using physical tools (mouses, screens and smartphones), and is experienced on physical technologies (computers and smartphones). Social media, then, is both digital and physical, and at the centre of cultures of social media are people.

Digital media scholars have implicitly demonstrated that social media is a powerful agent that has shaped communication, marketing and social practice, a force that enables new forms of participatory connection (Andrejevic, 2002;

Van Dijck et al., 2018). Despite this, museums in the twenty-first century have made little progress in collecting social media and indeed other forms of digital cultural heritage (Rees, 2021, p. 50). This is not to say that the work is not happening at all; rather, that a critical mass of museums have not taken up the task. Nevertheless, the limited representation of social media as museum objects in the scholarly literature suggests that museums are failing to recognise social media as museum objects or are challenged by the technical requirements for collecting – or both. What we do see in the literature, however, is that social media is more commonly understood as a tool deployed for online engagement (Drotner & Schrøder, 2013; Vassiliadis & Belenioti, 2017; Wilson-Barnao, 2022). Moreover, within the museum, social media is often understood as the purview of institutional marketing departments that employ it for communications, promotional purposes and public engagement activities (Wilson-Barnao, 2022). While this may be the case for many museums internationally, the landscape is changing, and museum professionals and some institutions have shifted and are shifting their ideas about the role of social media not only in museum practice but also in terms of its cultural value (Wilson-Barnao, 2022). So, despite the assumptions (and realities) of the already stated purposes of social media, it also operates as a space where everyday people share feelings, ideas and memories, often acting as an online diary of our lived experiences. In our private lives, it can be a place where we capture and share special moments such as a baby's first steps, high school graduations, a first job, the best party of our young lives and many others. In the online world, we create, share and carefully curate an account of our activities. Each post we make is a deliberate choice about what parts of our lives to display online, which develops what Alison Hearn (2008) describes as a form of digital self-branding. What we wear, where we visit and what we eat and do all contribute to the construction of an online identity.

In many ways, how people use social media is similar to the cabinets of curiosity or the 'wunderkammers' of the sixteenth century, where members of a privileged upper class would display prized objects, often dubiously collected on their travels, for public viewing (Williams & Tsien, 2013). These cabinets functioned to express certain aspects of the owner's life, including communicating social status and wealth. Similarly, people create content on social media feeds and then curate that content for an audience to engage with – the audience may comprise friends and family, but it may also include people who are completely unknown to the creator. The curation of content then conveys something of the person that they hope will be communicated or expressed – for example, when one shares a photo from a university graduation, there may be an intention to convey a feeling of pride while also communicating the new status that university qualifications might bring. When someone shares a photo of them and their partner kissing or in an embrace, they may want to share intangible feelings of love, joy and happiness. Similarly, when someone shares news of a relative's death, they may be at once making an announcement and, at the same time, sharing and processing grief. A key difference from the cabinets of curiosity is that we do not face the same material limitations as a museum does – purchasing and transportation costs, display space and distance from our audiences – when displaying content on social media. The objects we collect, create, display and interpret are both physical and/or digital in the online environment and are not restricted by earlier/previous limitations but rather governed only by our creativity and access to the internet. Likewise, audiences are not limited by geographic location or social and class circles. In social media display cabinets, creators can include as many objects as they like and, by using specific platforms (Facebook, Instagram TikTok and so on), enhance what is shared through the use of filters, music and other special effects. Each platform has its own culture and rules of engagement that inform what is produced and shared. Because of this, social media not only presents us with tools but also shapes how content is shared and with whom. In this way, all social media users become creators whose profiles are made available in cabinets of curiosity housed online. Within this context, this chapter considers the relationships that humans have with the digital world, especially social media, and what it means for museums to collect social media in an age when prosumers produce and consume content online.

Who is creating social media content?

Social media influencers are digital creators with large audiences on social media. They create content that aims to entertain, educate and market consumer products. Social media influencers differ from mainstream celebrities who use social media to connect more closely with their fanbase, which exists because of their work, profile or fame (Wilberforce, 2024). Social media influencers, on the other hand, intentionally set trends, collaborate with brands, spark dialogues and garner interest and buy-in from their audience on social media platforms (Alves de Castro et al., 2021). Social media influencing is increasingly becoming a viable form of employment, especially in commercial and marketing spheres, and the contributions of influencers to the development of social media are significant. Influencer content is not our sole focus here; instead, we use the term 'creator' rather than 'influencer' to acknowledge the importance of everyday people in producing content online, through social media platforms, as a way to document their lived experiences. We are led by Hank Green's original use of the term to refer to creators 'making all or part of their living making stuff on the internet, or are working toward that goal' (2016). Our understanding is also shaped by what Cunningham and Craig (2021) describe as 'creator culture,' which acknowledges the varying practices of creators and the differing affordances and governance structures of social media platforms. The term 'creator,' as we use it, describes individuals who produce creative content (such as photos, videos, sound recordings or text fragments), which is shared to generate attention on social media for an online audience or community. In *Understanding Celebrity* (2013), Graeme Turner uses the term 'the demotic turn' to describe the greater visibility of everyday people on reality TV and the reduced distance between what constitutes being ordinary and being a celebrity. The increased inclusion of ordinary people in contexts such as reality TV has fostered new forms of fame on technologies like social media. TikTok, for example, has had a significant impact in creating recognition that everyday people have a role to play in generating compelling content (Abidin, 2021). With this shift has come a proliferation of content that features a greater range of people who, while not always famous, participate in the production of online identities. Our use of the term 'creators' is intended to move discussion away from more conventional understandings of what is important on social media – the famous, the loudest and the most engaged with – towards one that better considers how museums can develop more representative collections that align with the civic obligation to document and record everyday life – and, in this case, the lives of creators who may or may not be considered influencers. Social media for these creators can present new opportunities for visibility, but this is accompanied by new challenges such as online trolling and data mining (Marwick et al., 2017); the complexities of such are important for museums to document.

It is important to acknowledge that some influencers can, and do, benefit museums by using their online networks to generate brand awareness and audience visitation. This is evidenced by the popularity of hashtags such as ArtTok and accounts such as @_theiconoclass, which has over 438,000 followers at the time of writing this book. The account is run by Australian TikTok creator Mary McGillivray, who draws on her expertise and skills to promote cultural discussions about art history and theory with online audiences engaged through a mainstream media agency, the ABC (Reich, 2021). Many artists have also become influencers. South African-born Australian artist CJ Hendry 'gained fame through social media, particularly Instagram, where she showcased her detailed drawings that often mimic the appearance of photographs.' (Delgado, 2023) With over 800,000 Instagram followers at the time of writing this book, the artist also uses social media in her art. One of the artist's projects was an international art scavenger hunt. For this project, Hendry created hyper-realistic drawings of other artists' work, then

> prints her drawings on t-shirts, packs them into bright red boxes labelled "Copyright Infringement/Trash Only", and sets out at the crack of dawn to leave them in public places, documented in her Instagram stories, for fans to come and find them
>
> (Cascone, 2023)

The use of social media in this project was crucial to its implementation and success. As these examples demonstrate, social media is a space where culture is produced, circulated and sold by a range of actors who use their digital skills to create products that they can then present online. Without doubt, the blurred line between artist, marketer, celebrity and historian challenges traditional distinctions and ways of working. However, our concern is with how social media might be used as a resource that can capture, memorialise and document everyday remarkable and unremarkable human experiences, not only as a tool of collection but also as intertwined with human experience and identity formation. While Kim Kardashian's posts, comprising staged portraits, brand collaborations and 'behind-the-scenes' glimpses, provide an insight into a high-profile person at a particular moment in the evolution of celebrity culture, this type of content is not our prime focus. Instead, we suggest that museums need to seek out everyday content if they are to build more representative collections. By 'everyday content' we mean the content produced by creators whose use of social media is often unthinkingly connected with their lived experience – not only those who use it for work, profile or influencing, whose content is of course important too, but also those who post, share and connect with friends, families and others in ways that might be regarded as unremarkable. In doing so, museums can present diverse accounts of important social history, lived experiences, major moments and events and so on. Collecting everyday social media will also work to preserve knowledge of the ways in which the social, cultural and political influence of the public internet and social media impacts people's lives. In saying this, we are not trying to make a value judgement about marketing as a cultural phenomenon – indeed, many museums collect marketing material as cultural artefacts. The National Museum of Australia, for example, holds a significant collection of marketing collateral (such as posters, t-shirts and badges) related to the 'Life. Be in it.' public health campaign (National Museum of Australia, 2023). Launched in Victoria in 1975 via a collaboration between advertising executive Phillip Adams and graphic designer Alexander Stitt, it is still considered one of Australia's most recognisable public health strategies. It told a compelling narrative about heavy-set protagonist Norm, who encouraged the nation to be more active through short, animated exercise skits. The campaign is nostalgic in the minds of many Australians, was influential in challenging the rise of obesity in Australia and holds prominent historical and cultural heritage status. By creating a distinction between social media influencers and creators, we intend to challenge the idea that influencers are the only players to create historically significant content online. We do not propose that museums do not collect influencer content; rather, we feel they need to pay attention to everyday material that delves deeper into the lived experiences of those who use social media. It is this kind of cultural collateral that we believe can say something profound about human existence; however, it is not currently being actively collected by museums.

In this context, creators are producers and prosumers who mediate everyday life using smartphones and other devices, and in doing so, they generate 'mediated memories' (van Dijck, 2007) in the form of social media content. This definition challenges contemporary understandings of what constitutes a memory object. Traditionally, when museums have collected objects, they have mostly consisted of static objects, such as letters or family photographs, which stand in for a particular memory event. It is the meaning attached to such objects, conceptually inscribed by their owners, that constitutes their significance. That is not to say that memory has not long been entwined with technologies. As van Dijck (2007, p. 39) explains, 'mediated memories are material triggers for future recall – produced through media technologies, whether pencil or camera.' Rather, contemporary memory objects are produced within a specific historical context, which in turn shapes our expression. Van Dijck's concept of mediated memories helps us to better understand social media as an object in its own right:

> Mediated memories are the activities and objects we produce and appropriate by means of media technologies, for creating and re-creating a sense of our past, present, and future of ourselves in relation to others.
>
> (van Dijck, 2007, p. 21)

In the contemporary era, creators use the tools provided by social platforms to represent themselves and to communicate against a backdrop of active and passive tracking – that is, the collection and creation of data about themselves. Similar to journalistic practices, the social media creator 'imagines' their audience and communicates with them 'according to the norms that they perceive to be generally accepted' (boyd, 2007, p. 3). Interestingly, this means that creators can produce more expressive content than in previous eras, such as using music to convey a particular emotion or filters to make more engaging content. Wearable sensors in the form of smartwatches or other devices also play a role in layering additional meaning into these social media objects. Self-tracking has become 'an essential element of the work of remembering' (Lyall, 2024, p. 1). For example, users of watches share information about weight, blood pressure or exercise routines on social media, with this content helping to represent an individual's identity. Creators benefit from their digital labour by gaining exposure, as do digital media platforms that monetise this engagement (Carah, 2014). The presentation of self on social media is an integral part of capitalism and its search for new forms of value (Hearn, 2010). While algorithms shape how creators are presented, creators do express agency over how they make and present themselves (Bhandari & Bimo, 2022). Craig and Cunningham (2019, p. 5) use the terms 'social media entertainment' or 'SME' to acknowledge the emergence 'of amateur content creators using new entertainment and communicative formats, including vlogging, gameplay, and do-it-yourself (DIY), to develop potentially sustainable businesses based on significant followings that can extend across multiple platforms.' Creators can start out as 'hobbyists … with little intention of developing any form of income, let alone a sustainable career.' (Craig & Cunningham, 2019, p. 11) Therefore, creators, as we understand them, produce amateur content on social media platforms where it can amplify discussions on different global topics and issues, providing an insight into community sentiment, or alternatively, document important political or historical events.

The definitions provided here, while not comprehensive, help us to understand the complexity of who is creating content on social media and their intentions. This alerts museums to the diversity of users and asks them to think more critically about those people. Not all content is produced in the same context by the same kinds of people, and this will continue to change as social media is further embedded into the lives of generations of people who will have always had access to social media platforms.

What can social media tell us about life?

The rise of social media is undeniable. It has changed the ways we connect, communicate and participate in life. Beyond being a form of digital production, social media is a means of connectivity and networking, entertainment and leisure, employment and business, activism and social change and identity formation. As digital literacy evolves and the use of platforms expands, so will the societal functionality of social media. Social media platforms are changing, such as the rebranding of the well-known platform of Twitter to X under the leadership of Elon Musk, and new platforms that mimic the functionality of that platform have emerged, including Meta's Threads and Bluesky, a platform created by Twitter's original founder. While understanding social media platforms, their specificities, functionalities and communities are important for museums when collecting social media – especially if they want to understand the impact on everyday lives – it is not necessarily productive in this book to focus on the platforms of today. Instead, we want to zoom out to the social and cultural aspects of what social media, and its many incarnations, have meant for individuals and groups. Within this ever-changing context, we have identified six social and cultural outputs of social media that are shaping and being shaped by our use of social media.

Connectivity and communication (ephemeral personal collections)

Social media itself has heralded new ways of connecting with family, friends, colleagues and strangers, contributing to the way we perceive reality. Ordinary people create collections of personal photos and videos on privately owned social media platforms such as Facebook and YouTube, where they manage the presentation of self. Examples of this type of content are collections of baby photographs or remembrance profiles dedicated to people who have passed away. Personal photos and home movies are uploaded for the purpose of sharing with private networks. Acting as an ever-evolving life log, this content can provide rich detail about individual biographies (Marshall, 2018), and associated data, such as friends and connections, can provide important context. By drawing on the frame of connectivity and communication, we seek to highlight the availability of information that is useful for historical research, as it can present rich detail about an individual and their relationships. This category also encompasses messaging applications and the variety of ways in which we use social media to connect.

Sharing and expression (digital intimacy)

By sharing and expression, we refer to the online identity practices of creators who create content and curate their identity online, enabling new forms of digital proximity and intimacy. Information and emotions that are usually exchanged with friends or family in 'zones of familiarity' (Berlant, 1998) are expressed with multiple audiences on platforms. Dobson et al. (2018) describe 'digital intimate publics' as

> sometimes proximate to, witness to, and called or "tagged" to others, sometimes effusive, expressions of love, pleasure, pain, suffering, and need from a network of friends, colleagues, acquaintances, family members, and others in a digital network with whom we are close and not so close.

In other words, social media allows creators to seek out new forms of visibility, intimacy and connection. Key to the creation of this type of content is the authentic public performance of identity online, which includes additional intimate forms of expression that extend beyond more routine forms of communication. This can include creators providing emotional confessions, expressing their grief, giving thoughtful monologues or engaging in exchanges about how individuals navigate public life. For example, an individual might discuss how they navigate their sexual orientation or weight loss.

Visual vocabulary (remix culture)

This category refers to memes and emojis, and other types of visual signals that create meaning between social media users. These visual symbols 'seldom preserve a sense of ownership' and 'rarely give credit'; nor is there an expectation of a need for 'permission' (Marshall & Shipman, 2019, p. 96). Drawing on Lessig (2008), museum studies scholar Arran Rees (2021) uses the term 'remix museology' to highlight the emerging nature of collecting and the need for museums to adjust their practices to accommodate these types of objects. Often, the objects are not owned by any one person and are used as collective symbols to express a particular feeling or attitude. The 'hang in there' cat meme is a notable example of this, as it stands in for many people's experiences of sentiment about surviving a difficult situation. These objects are important to collect because meme circulation between multiple users tells us something about how people living in our time feel about a particular experience. Due to distributed authorship, these objects present challenges to collecting institutions.

Intangible heritage (reviving the past)

The category of intangible heritage incorporates the use of social media to preserve traditions and practices. This might involve users posting videos or photos of traditional approaches to dressing or cooking. It also encompasses social channels dedicated to remembering a particular era or cultural experience – for example, growing up in the 1990s. Users share anecdotes and media content to remember the past, preserve it or create a sense of community. In an increasingly digital world, this category also catches new and emerging intangible heritage that might take place only on social media or the internet, rather than being bound only by representing physical tradition online.

News, entertainment and information (novel infotainment)

This category refers to new forms of news and entertainment, which are now created and distributed using social media, such as local news, along with other forms of entertainment and information generated both by institutions and creators. It acknowledges that news, entertainment and information are now consumed beyond legacy media outlets (television, radio and newspapers). In some cases, news media agencies operate exclusively on social media platforms. In addition, social media influencers and creators create and deliver digital performances on social media, which are consumed by users for entertainment. This can also entail citizens reporting from the frontlines where international journalists are banned.

Business and branding (algorithms and advertising)

In participatory digital environments, users draw on inbuilt forms of branding to create content that embeds marketing into interpersonal communication. These devices include sponsored filters and lenses. Snapchat, for instance, offered a lens that allowed users to create a Disney Pixar-type character, which could then be shared on other social media platforms. The purpose of this category is to acknowledge social media's capacity for advertising purposes. This also entails the use of marketing and audience research to microtarget individuals. Examples here include the everyday use of data collected by social media algorithms for microtargeting. This category also includes data-sharing and selling practices that may need to be accounted for when collecting a social object of this nature.

Societal impact and activism

Our response to societal issues is not only shaped by legacy media but also by the depictions of creators on social channels that frame broader understandings and approaches to issues (Abidin et al., 2020). This form of activism can be targeted at political parties and politicians, but is also used to target corporations and institutions. A personal post from a significant event, such as #BlackLivesMatter or #MeToo, can reflect social unrest and a particular movement at a specific point in time. Such posts are representative of forms of everyday activism performed by networked publics that capture shifting social values and broader political unrest. Other examples include uprisings such as the Arab Spring and content documenting upheavals, demonstrations, social violence or insurgencies. It can also involve online advocacy for causes such as the environment. Social activism is experienced, exchanged and activated by individuals and communities using digital means and can demonstrate collectives attempting to change a particular regime or talk back to power.

While the above list is not exhaustive and will continue to evolve as the culture of digital experience changes, it is clear that social media entertains us, gives us our news and can also tell us about the way people think and feel about important issues. Social media can assist museums in creating more diverse and representative collections, seeking out objects and stories from under-represented communities and disadvantaged groups whose experiences are increasingly online and outside of the mainstream contexts from which many museums continue to collect. Social media is important historically and culturally, yet one of the biggest challenges for museums is what to collect, not only from the perspective of social media as a large and unwieldy corpus of information, but from the perspective of 'objectness.'

What is a social media object?

All kinds of people create social media content – in fact, an estimated five billion people use social media globally (Wong, 2024). With over half the world's population creating and sharing content, it is understandably complex to describe what a social media object is. To frame our thinking, we regard the content housed on social media as born-digital objects and draw on the United Nations Educational, Scientific and Cultural Organisation's (UNESCO) Charter on the Preservation of Digital Heritage (2003, p. 1) and understand social media as capturing 'unique resources of human knowledge and expression.' At the same time, social media fits neatly within UNESCO's definition of intangible heritage, given that it is

> transmitted from generation to generation, is constantly recreated by communities and groups in response to their environment, their interaction with nature and their history, and provides them with a sense of identity and continuity, thus promoting respect for cultural diversity and human creativity.
>
> (UNESCO, 2003, p. 4)

In this way, intangible cultural heritage is not only being presented on social media by cultural actors but also being created on social media by native users, forging new and exciting immaterial cultural expressions.

More than only an object type (e.g., furniture, paintings, tools), it is social media's intangible aspects that are integral to understanding its materiality, which is necessarily complex. Despite this, certain characteristics of social media can be identified to place some parameters around what museums can understand to be social media objects and what might fall outside such boundaries. First and foremost, a social media object requires its publication to an online platform designed for social engagement. Without its publication, publicly or privately, objects that we might understand as social media lose their status because it is the sharing of content and the engagement with content that ascribe such media its social nature in the online sphere. For example, a video can be produced on a smartphone and kept by its owner on that same device, archived in a similar way to a photograph in a photo album, and looked back on by the owner as a memory (van Dijck, 2007). This video, while born-digital, is not a social media object. If the owner subsequently posts this video to their Facebook account, it acquires a different status as a social media object because its posting applies a layer of meaning to the object that defines it as social. A museum could collect this video as either a born-digital object and/or as a social media object. The reasons why a museum might collect this video in different contexts will be determined by a range of factors, including its sharing on social media related to its significance, for example, if the video went viral, made an impact in a community, or is connected to a broader movement or issue. Regardless, it is important to note that while the video may be technically the same (noting that its publication on social media potentially changes its formatting and size), its status as a social media object relies on its publication to a social media platform. It is the intangible aspects of social media – intention and engagement – that become important in assessing what is and is not social media.

In the current landscape of digital products, social media objects might incorporate video recordings, photographs, digital artworks and text. They may also encapsulate music, filters and other information, such as metadata. Much like the choices, tools and paints of an artist, these different elements of social media objects hold within them insights into the intention of the creator. Furthermore, because a social media object relies on its publication to an online platform, we need to consider other aspects of the platforms that add meaning to these objects. This includes the visual environment in which the post was published – for example, the media platform's design and architecture, which provides knowledge of how a social media object was disseminated by a creator, and received and engaged with by other creators. This, of course, can vary depending on whether the social media object was consumed on a desktop computer or a smartphone. Additionally, the brand of such devices (Apple, Samsung, Microsoft and so on) impacts how content is received and viewed online. Moreover, a social media object's sociality is often demonstrated by creator responses – that is, the meaning created by the interaction between creators, which is facilitated by social media platforms. Therefore, likes, comments, reposting, remixing and so on become important aspects of the composition of a social media object.

What all this means is that social media objects are complex and diverse and can materialise in a vast range of shapes and appearances. With most physical object types – for example, a trophy – no matter how simply or ornately designed, they generally take the same shape. Likewise, regardless of its form, a hat comprises similar material qualities that determine its status in that category. Social media objects, on the other hand, will look different yet may share many commonalities with other object types at the same time. For example, a core element of a social media object may be a video – some videos will be social media objects and others will not. This all depends on their context. Some social media objects will be extracted files, while others will be recordings or copies of what is available online – neither is less valuable than the other. All this will complicate logic in museums, especially in the catalogue, as museums draw on thesauruses that focus on physical and simple born-digital object categories. Nevertheless, it will be important to create a category of object that is social media, to be able to discover and provide access to such objects for research and engagement purposes.

How does collecting social media impact museum practices?

The introduction of social media as an object type and a focus of collecting in museums will necessarily require museums to revisit and review their policies, practices and infrastructures to create an environment in which the collecting of social media can be successful. While the practices, policies and infrastructures required for the collecting of physical objects do not necessarily require alteration, new practices, processes and infrastructures will be required to embed social media collecting into the institution. As with physical collecting, it is important that the museum's collection strategy is clearly defined and sits comfortably next to other policies and practices. Articulating social media as an object type or focus within a collecting strategy will help shape curatorial decisions, along with organisational decisions about the technical infrastructure required to support collecting activities and staff training and workflows. While this is extremely important and is a good starting point, there are more practical challenges facing museum professionals when identifying and collecting social media.

Many museums will receive offers from individuals and groups to donate or sell their physical objects. In addition, through their research, museum curators might identify individuals and groups who have been associated with specific historical moments, events or experiences and approach individuals and organisations to learn more about their stories and identify potentially significant physical objects through those encounters. Alongside more serendipitous ways in which museum collecting takes place, the practices of collecting physical objects in museums have been well documented (Knell, 2004; Macdonald, 2006; Matassa, 2011). These practices sit within a framework of cultural and social understanding about the role of museums and objects as collections that has permeated public knowledge. Therefore, there is a wide understanding that physical objects are important to history-making practices and institutions in societies (Pearce, 1994). On the flip side, the idea that social media is important to history and that the content created on social media platforms is important to memory-making institutions has not yet taken hold. Museums, for example, are not being approached by social media creators with offers to collect their social media objects, nor are museum professionals generally prioritising the identification of individual users engaging in moments or events of historical significance and seeking out their social media objects and archives. This is not to say that it is not happening – indeed, there is good work being done – but rather that museums and societies still do not consider social media as important as a cultural collection in its own right. Even without this tacit recognition, the importance of social media can be witnessed playing out every day, including creators making political statements and individuals, including current and former heads of state, high-profile activists like Greta Thunberg and celebrities using social media to comment on significant local, regional and international political and social issues. This kind of social media content might make news headlines, be referenced in articles and books, and thus be considered important, which should signal to museums the importance of the objects being produced and repurposed. What those who are not participating in social media are less likely to see or access are the everyday, seemingly ordinary creators whose use of social media can document how the public internet has shaped identity formation and human connectivity. This is a worthy role museums can and should take in communicating the human value of social media to identity formation and everyday lived experiences. However, if people who own their social media content are not understanding its objectness and are not offering their social media objects to museums, museums must take a more active approach to collecting social media.

There are many different ways in which museum professionals can approach identifying content to collect. The most straightforward way involves manually searching various media platforms using inbuilt search functions. This approach can be useful to foster familiarisation with each platform's content specificity/type; however, it comes with the risk of doom scrolling or of only viewing content that falls within personal algorithmic bubbles. Herein lies the biggest challenge in general, as each search creates data informing what content is reflected in a user's feed, so what might commence as a broad field of social media is constantly narrowed and delimited by search terms, likes, views, dwell time and so on. This means there is some content, based on one's own preferences, that may never be seen. This, of course, suggests that the inherent bias of social media collecting is informed by the ways in which the platform interacts with users, and vice versa. Curators could attempt to train algorithms through a research process whereby one likes, comments and shares relevant content that intentionally shifts an algorithm to present content that might be more aligned with collecting intentions or the focus area of a museum. This may uncover content that is relevant; however, this approach suggests the ability to focus on one topic area at any one time, with a need to retrain the algorithm, which may take some time, and with little knowledge of how the previous area of interest informs the new one. In an attempt to search for content related to intersex communities, we used the search engines of Facebook, X (formerly Twitter) and YouTube to identify content that was created and posted by creators identifying as intersex. In doing so, we discovered that using straightforward search terms such as 'intersex' returned a large number of social media posts that we will call 'explainer' posts. A majority, if not all, of the content viewed consisted of posts that contained photos, videos and the like that explained this term, sometimes from those who identified as part of the intersex group and sometimes not. We struggled to find content created by those who identified as intersex that communicated something of their lived experience in a personalised or diarised way. Of course, this is only one example of a search attempt; however, it does suggest that access to content is limited by the search functionality of platforms comprising different levels of complexity and is dependent on the user's own histories of engagement on the platforms.

While searching through social media platforms as described above may be beneficial and indeed will support curators and others to identify specific collections, it would be useful for museums that intend to collect social media to define their collecting parameters. Some of this will be taken care of in higher-level policies and frameworks; however, to make the most of human resources, it can be helpful to further define the field to ensure efficiency. This is not unlike setting parameters for targeted collecting in a physical sense. That is deciding who, what, where, why and when you are collecting in relation to a specific topic of interest. This practice does not imply the need to know exactly what objects are to be collected, but rather involves narrowing a focus to a key area of significance through which you can map the actors, ideas and nuances and work towards identifying objects of significance in what is a large and unwieldy online space.

In a social media context, this intention-setting might involve identifying a particular platform or creator and following their pages, distinguishing and using hashtags and becoming familiar with the language associated with the community of interest to inform search terms. It is also imperative to identify whether the museum wants to collect more permanent content, like a post or a tweet that can be downloaded and/or captured in a range of ways over time, or if the intention is to collect 'ephemeral content' such as Instagram, Facebook or Snapchat stories and reels, which may only be visible for 24 hours – the latter being a complicated proposition from a practice perspective, as it will likely involve a serendipitous interaction. As a computer scientist and archivist, Catherine Marshall (2018, p. 258) points out, 'digital media may radically change our sense of ephemera' as we preserve more of it in different ways – for example, 'handwritten letters have all but vanished from our everyday lives' and, unlike in paper-based communication, on social media, we have access to both sides of a correspondence chain. The search will be guided by whether it is setting out to collect one or multiple objects and by consideration of how they will be displayed. It can be helpful to decide at the onset of the process whether it is worth collecting users' interactions, such as comments on posts, and whether to include associated metadata that might help with demonstrating a particular post's importance. Of course, it is challenging to answer all these questions before identifying collections.

Regardless of how museums go about identifying social media to collect, it is important for these institutions and those responsible for collecting social media to gain a stronger understanding of the 'structure of born-digital objects and their specific reliance on distributed technical infrastructures' (Arrigoni & McKim, 2022, p. 13). To do this, museums need to experiment with this form of collecting. Compiling social media requires museums to think and make assumptions about how much they expect their digital collection to grow, whether they will collect in both digital and physical formats and how much access museum publics will get to this content. Additional considerations include how to acknowledge the intellectual property rights of content creators, the ongoing maintenance of IT systems required to support this approach and where data will be stored and how often such data will be backed up. What this means is that museums must be prepared to revisit and alter their existing practices, examine the allocation of their resources and take an active approach to collecting social media.

Applying curatorial and collection logics to social media

To further cement our point that social media is worthy of being included in museum collections, we have identified the following examples that demonstrate the capacity of social media and its context to be considered historically significant in their own right and that help us to identify where it might find a philosophical place in a museum collection. The task of applying curatorial and collecting logics to creator content on social media enhances our understanding of why collecting social media is critical.

Chronicles of war

Valeria Shashenok (@Valerisssh) was 20 years old when she started documenting her own account of the Russian invasion of Ukraine on TikTok (Nilsson-Julien, 2023). While not intending to position herself as a creator with a following of over 1.3 million on TikTok and 111,000 on Instagram, her posts gained popularity as a result of her social content, which captured how she navigated the destruction of her hometown. Living underground with her parents, pet dog and two family friends, the young creator documents the everyday adjustments that she and her family had to make to live through the crisis, ranging from what they cooked and bought at the supermarket to the destruction of the buildings in her neighbourhood. Her posts solicit a strong and emotional response that resonates with the experience of a young person bound to a shelter for 24 hours a day. The creator's observations often humorously capture her reality – for example, in one post, she cooks pasta in the bomb shelter while she imagines that she has escaped to Italy, and in others, she depicts the horrors of war, showing the destruction of bombed buildings. Shashenok's content is a strong example of the category of "sharing and expression (digital intimacy)" because her social media posts work to form a strong emotional connection that invites her followers to connect with her personal experience. In contrast to much of the fake news distributed on social media platforms during this time, Shashenok's content appears to offer an authentic look at her experiences of the war in Ukraine. In a museum context, collecting a number of @Valerisssh social media posts could literally document a first-hand account of the war from a Ukrainian perspective. The war continues to be a major international conflict of the twentieth century, and as such, is significant for museums to document. Alongside this, the use of social media itself is important. Without social media, Shashenok's experience could have been lost or obscured in history. Social media has welcomed great visibility through online communication methods that have created a space for a seemingly ordinary Ukrainian citizen to share her experiences of conflict in real time, regardless of her profile or status offline. The intentions of Shashenok are equally as important: Her sometimes humorous and sometimes deeply concerning posts support her role as an activist who believed that the realities of what was happening, sometimes overlooked by the media, needed to be shared, and social media created a global online space for this to occur.

#TwoMenKissing

On 12 June 2016, 29-year-old Omar Mateen murdered 49 people and wounded 53 more in a mass shooting at Pulse, a gay nightclub in Orlando, Florida, in the United States. The shooting is considered one of the deadliest terrorist attacks in the United States since the September 11 terrorist attacks of 2001. This event is of historical significance locally in Orlando, to Lesbian, Gay, Bisexual, Transgender, Intersex and Queer + (LGBTIQ+) communities locally and internationally, and to the world in the context of ongoing and increased terrorism. Mateen's father told reporters that his son had become enraged by the sight of two men kissing, which may have informed his actions that night. Soon after this news was reported, the hashtag #TwoMenKissing was created and used on social media to accompany images of men kissing men. The images contained in the posts were often supplemented by words condemning violence against LGBTIQ+ people and communities and advocating for LGBTIQ+ rights. Scott McKinnon (2016) explains that in Western countries such as the United States and Australia, where variant sexualities are increasingly accepted, public displays of affection, including holding hands and kissing, continue to carry risks for many. He says the gay kiss has a long history of censorship, regardless of the moves that have taken place to increase social inclusion of same-sex practices in public. Within this context, the hashtag #TwoMenKissing and the visual and textual elements of each post work to highlight discrimination against gay men while acting as a platform for LGBTIQ+ advocacy in general. Alongside this, #TwoMenKissing presents the role of social media and online creators in online activism, a form of activism whereby non-traditional activists – such as those who attend protests and rallies – can participate in online conversations about challenging social, political and cultural issues in new ways. If a museum were to collect a representative sample of posts from #TwoMenKissing, it could not only share an important story of a horrific and tragic event but would also position the social media object in the wider cultural contexts of LGBTIQ+ rights and activism and online activism more generally.

Beyond the role of social media in changing the way we operate in the world is the relationship humans have with social media that makes content and social media objects even more meaningful to the project of documenting human experiences and worthy of museums' attention. In a 2021 interview in *The Guardian*, proud Erub and non-binary person Nich Richie explained their relationship with the social media platform TikTok. They said, 'I didn't have ready access to information growing up … I didn't know anything about Indigenous people's culture. I didn't know about activism. I didn't get to see myself on any platform' (Boseley, 2021). Richie grew up in a non-Indigenous household, which resulted in a disconnection from their country and community. Richie explains that downloading the social media application TikTok was transformative in their identity journey, enabling them to discover a huge number of First Nations content creators online. They explained: 'It helped me in my process of reconnection to culture, because beforehand I was very much struggling' (Boseley, 2021). Richie found their community on the TikTok platform, and now their status as a content creator is all part of Richie's identity formation as a First Nations Australian, a non-binary person and a human living in the twenty-first century.

The above examples identify objects that could be collected by museums – video content, photos, text fragments and so on. These examples were identified through a curatorial lens. But why social media? Some curators may be wondering why a museum wouldn't collect one of the outfits that Valeria Shashenok wore in one of her videos or a piece of rubble from around the site of her family's bunker. While the physical artefacts of war, and life in general, have and will continue to have an important place in museum collecting, without social media, Shashenok may not have been able to communicate her story as widely or in real time. It is her intention, informed by social justice, to share the realities of her situation with the world, which makes this story meaningful. It is also the responses of those who engaged, online and through media outlets, that make this story worthy. It is the role of social media in changing the way humans communicate and connect across time and geography that makes this story an integral part of contemporary life. Because the social media element is so entwined with the meaning of the object – as a tool, as a mode of communication, as a gathering space – collecting the social media object, rather than other objects, becomes important in the telling and re-telling of this story for generations to come.

Conclusion

In this chapter, we have articulated the value of social media to society and to museums. This included defining social media as internet-based technologies that create opportunities for social networking, yet are always entwined with our material worlds. Within the context of museums collecting social media, we defined a distinction between creators and influencers – creators being everyday makers of content on and for social media, and influencers having more of a public profile, often associated with celebrity and/or work. In doing so, everyday social media – that of creators – is highlighted as a key focus for museums, to ensure that collections of social media recognise not only the influencers and their influence but also the everyday impact of social media on people's lives.

The chapter outlined what social media can tell us about society and culture and how creator content intersects with communication, digital intimacy, remix culture, intangible cultural heritage and more. The societal and cultural role of social media makes it important for museums to pay attention to and collect museum objects. We proposed six categories designed to assist practitioners when determining the types of social media objects worthy of collecting. Social media objects in this context are thus a unique yet complex object type. This chapter is by no means encyclopaedic but rather outlines many of the considerations that will support museums and their professionals to build an awareness of the many and varied ways people use and engage with social media, and thus where links exist between social media and museum collecting remits.

Insights from practitioners

Seb Chan

> There is no [single] creator. The creator is creating with the platform and the network and everybody else to deliver what you see at the other end.

Seb Chan, Director and CEO of the Australian Centre for the Moving Image (ACMI), offered us strong perspectives on collecting social media in museums. Over the course of his career, Seb has helped museums and other cultural institutions adapt to a changing world, especially through the critical and creative adoption of emerging technologies and concepts, including open access, mass collaboration, web metrics and digital engagement.

Context over content

Seb emphasised that, for him and ACMI, the value of social media lies not in individual posts or videos (the content), but in the contextual ecosystem that informs how people engage with the internet and social media. The social platform, its interface and user interactions all play a role in shaping this meaning. Social media objects, therefore, are 'like a mirror with a thousand reflective faces.' The content alone is insufficient without its platform context – that is what makes it social media. Seb highlighted, for example, that certain features, such as TikTok's Duet function, create entirely new forms of media that cannot be separated from the platform's design. Collecting just the video aspects of content produced through the Duet function is inadequate, and he again stressed the importance of the interface and user experience as significant to the object's meaning.

Collecting the ugly

Seb advocates strongly for collaborative collecting across cultural institutions. In his view, different museums collect the same object but use it to tell different stories based on their specific missions and collecting priorities. Digital objects provided museums with opportunities to do this kind of collecting because what is on the internet can be replicated – signalling the unique nature of digital objects. Furthermore, he argues for the importance of collecting not just the polished or popular, which is often perceived as the most compelling content, because it is the loudest – but also the difficult, controversial or ephemeral aspects of digital life – what he calls 'the horrors,' which exist in spades on social media. So, if museums want to collect in order to better represent digital life, related objects need to be complex, nuanced and diverse.

Arran Rees

> We're not going to find shoe boxes of photos under beds anymore, it's all on Facebook.

Arran Rees, Museum Data Manager at the Collections Trust (UK) and museum researcher and practitioner, discussed with us his work on collecting digital cultural heritage, particularly social media content and memes. His research explores the complexities of curating digital objects, the evolving role of curators and the institutional challenges of preserving ephemeral digital culture. Arran has completed a PhD on the topic as well as engaging in collaborative projects with institutions including the Science Museum and the National Science and Media Museum.

Curatorial intent shapes the object

Different collecting institutions have different remits. For example, design museums may focus on social media interfaces, while social history museums will likely prioritise social media content and stories. In addition, the way a social media object is collected defines what it becomes in a museum context. Arran explained that curators effectively 'create' digital objects through the decisions they make about what to capture and how, signalling the important role of curatorial work in determining collecting methodologies.

Social media objects are dynamic

Arran emphasised that digital objects, in contrast to physical ones, are not inherently tangible or fixed. Internet memes, for example, are not static images but rather are contextual and dynamic – they change with every user interaction, comment, like and reshare. Furthermore, to fully understand memes as museum objects requires an understanding of the platform on which they were shared, the logics of that platform and the visual and/or virtual environment, including functionality.

Museums or archives?

Through his work and research, Arran found that memes and other digital artefacts often fit better in archival structures than within traditional museum collections due to their layered, interconnected nature. Archives collection management allows for ongoing accrual and contextual updates, which he believes are crucial for evolving digital content. Museums will need to shift their collection-management practices if they want to collect social media objects that continue to be dynamic and changing, and connected to their live online contexts.

References

Abidin, C. (2021). Mapping internet celebrity on TikTok: Exploring attention economies and visibility labours. *Cultural Science Journal, 12*(1), 77–103. https://doi.org/10.5334/csci.140

Abidin, C., Brockington, D., Goodman, M., Mostafanezhad, M., & Richey, L. (2020). The tropes of celebrity environmentalism. *Annual Review of Environment and Resources, 45*, 387–410. https://doi.org/10.1146/annurev-environ-012320-081703

Alves de Castro, C., O'Reilly, I., & Carthy, A. (2021). Social media influencers (SMIs) in context: A literature review. *Journal of Marketing Management, 9*(2), 59–71.

Andrejevic, M. (2002). The work of being watched: Interactive media and the exploitation of self-disclosure. *Critical Studies in Media Communication, 19*(2): 230–248. https://doi.org/10.1080/07393180216561

Arrigoni, G., & McKim, J. (2022). Experimentation and collecting practice: Balancing flexible policies and accountability in developing born-digital museum collections. *Museum Management and Curatorship, 39*(3), 317–334. https://doi.org/10.1080/09647775.2022.2133782

Berlant, L. (1998). Intimacy: A special issue. *Critical Inquiry, 24*(2), 281–288. https://www.jstor.org/stable/1344169

Bhandari, A., & Bimo, S. (2022). Why's everyone on TikTok now? The algorithmized self and the future of self-making on social media. *Social Media + Society, 8*(1). https://doi.org/10.1177/20563051221086241

Boseley, M. (2021, 10 July) 'I found my identity': How TikTok is changing the lives of its popular Indigenous creators. *The Guardian*, Accessed 11 January 2024 from www.theguardian.com/australia-news/2021/jul/10/i-found-my-identity-how-tiktok-is-changing-the-lives-of-its-popular-indigenous-creators

boyd, d. (2007). Social network sites: Public, private, or what? *Knowledge Tree, 13*. Accessed 16 February 2025 from http://kt.flexiblelearning.net.au/tkt2007/?page_id=28

Carah, N. (2014). Curators of databases: Circulating images, managing attention and making value on social media. *Media International Australia, 150*, 137–142. https://doi.org/10.1177/1329878X1415000125

Carr, C. T., & Hayes, R. A. (2015). Social media: Defining, developing, and divining. *Atlantic Journal of Communication, 23*(1), 46–65. https://doi.org/10.1080/15456870.2015.972282

Cascone, S. (2023). Artist CJ Hendry's wildly popular art scavenger hunt is the subject of a new documentary that captures the thrill of the chase. artnet. Accessed 16

February 2025 from https://news.artnet.com/art-world/cj-hendry-copyright-infringement-documentary-2262538
Craig, D., & Cunningham, S. (2019). *Social media entertainment: The new intersection of Hollywood and Silicon Valley*. New York University Press.
Cunningham, S. & Craig, D. (2021). *Creator culture: An introduction to global social media entertainment*. New York University Press.
Delgado, M. (2023). CJ Hendry. Patreon. Accessed 15 June 2025 from www.patreon.com/posts/cj-hendry-94711157?l=de
Dobson, A. S., Carah, N., & Robards, B. (2018). Digital intimate publics and social media: Towards theorising public lives on private platforms. In A. S. Dobson, B. Robards, & N. Carah (Eds.), *Digital intimate publics and social media* (pp. 3–27). Palgrave Macmillan.
Drotner, K., & Schrøder, K. (2013). *Museum communication and social media: The connected museum*. Routledge.
Green, H. (2016, 16 June). Introducing the internet creators guild. *Medium*. Accessed 15 June 2025 from https://medium.com
Hearn, A. (2008). 'Meat, mask, burden': Probing the contours of the branded 'self'. *Journal of Consumer Culture*, *8*(2), 197–217. https://doi.org/10.1177/1469540508090086
Hearn, A. (2010). Structuring feeling: Web 2.0, online ranking and rating, and the digital 'reputation' economy. *Ephemera: Theory & Politics in Organization*, *10*, 421–438. https://ephemerajournal.org/sites/default/files/2022-01/10-3ephemeranov10.pdf
Knell, S. (2004). *Museums and the future of collecting*. Routledge.
Lessig, L. (2008). *Remix: Making art and commerce thrive in the hybrid economy*. Bloomsbury.
Lyall, B. (2024). Narratives in numbers: Sociotechnical storytelling with self-tracking. *Memory, Mind & Media*, *3*, 1–20. https://doi.org/10.1017/mem.2023.12
Macdonald, S. (2006). *A companion to museum studies*. Blackwell.
Marshall, C. (2018). *Writing for social media*. BCS.
Marshall, C., & Shipman, F. (2019). The ownership and control of online photos and game data: Patterns, trends, and keeping pace with evolving circumstances. *ACM/IEEE Joint Conference on Digital Libraries*. https://doi.org/10.1109/JCDL.2019.00022
Marwick, A., Fontaine, C., & boyd, d. (2017). 'Nobody sees it, nobody gets mad': Social media, privacy, and personal responsibility among low-SES youth. *Social Media and Society*, *3*(2). https://doi.org/10.1177/2056305117710455
Matassa, F. (2011). *Museum collections management*. Facet Publishing.
McKinnon, S. (2016, 16 June). Why are we still scared of seeing two men kissing? *The Conversation*. Accessed 16 February 2025 from https://theconversation.com/why-are-we-still-scared-of-seeing-two-men-kissing-61085
National Museum of Australia. (2023). Life. Be in it. Launch. Accessed 3 February 2024 from www.nma.gov.au/defining-moments/resources/life-be-in-it-launch
Nilsson-Julien, E. (2023, 1 July). Valeria Shashenok went viral on the social media platform after posting video clips of the damage caused by Russian bombings. *Euronews*. Accessed 16 February 2025 from www.euronews.com/2023/01/07/meet-the-ukrainian-tiktok-star-documenting-life-in-her-war-torn-homeland
Pearce, S. (1994). *Interpreting objects and collections*. Routledge.
Rees, A. (2021). Remixing museology: An approach to collecting social media in museums. PhD thesis, University of Leeds.
Reich, H. (2021). Australian TikTok creator Mary McGillivray brings art history to a Gen Z audience as _theiconoclass. *The Art Show*, ABC TV. Accessed 16 February 2025 from www.abc.net.au/news/2021-08-22/arttok-australian-art-history-tik-tok-theiconoclass/100227190
Turner, G. (2013). *Understanding celebrity*. Sage.

UNESCO. (2003) Charter of the preservation of digital heritage. Accessed 27 January 2023 from https://www.unesco.org/en/legal-affairs/charter-preservation-digital-heritage
van Dijck, J. (2007). *Mediated memories in the digital age*. Stanford University Press.
van Dijck, J., Poell, T., & De Waal, M. (2018). *The platform society: Public values in a connective world*. Oxford University Press.
Vassiliadis, C., & Belenioti, Z. (2017). Museums and cultural heritage via social media: An integrated literature review. *Tousismos*, *12*(3), 97–132.
Wilberforce, D. (2024). Social media: Revolutionizing celebrity culture in 2024. *Medium*. Accessed 15 June 2025 from https://medium.com/the-orange-journal/social-media-revolutionizing-celebrity-culture-in-2024-5cab2b8968a7
Williams, T., & Tsien, B. (2013). *Wunderkammer*. Yale University Press.
Wilson-Barnao, C. (2022). *Digital access and museums as platforms*. Routledge.
Wong, B. (2024). Top social media statistics and trends of 2024. *Forbes Advisor*. Accessed 23 February 2025 from www.forbes.com/advisor/business/social-media-statistics

3 Significance and social media

When thinking about collecting social media objects, the first hurdle is the sheer amount of information available on the internet. Using any search engine will return hundreds if not thousands of results – from traditional, authoritative and trusted sources to opinions, imaginings and misinformation. Digital anthropologist Giles Crouch says the internet is a 'messy, chaotic, unruly mess' (Crouch, 2022). Crouch's description can be applied to a wide range of different internet contexts, including news media, streaming services, cryptocurrency and more. If the internet is an experiment that is constantly changing, perhaps it will always be chaotic, yet as Crouch explains, the internet is 'the first global scale sociocultural system humans have ever built. It is, in a way, magical.' This makes the internet significant to human experience and, therefore, to human history. Its significance means the internet, and its many faces, including social media, are important socially and culturally and thus something to which museums must pay attention as historically significant and worthy of collecting. But how do museums begin to think through what to collect from the vast and chaotic corpus of the internet?

Perhaps the most important practice associated with the role of the curator in a museum is that of identifying and assessing the significance of things – that is, the determining of meaning, relevance and context, and arguing why something is important as it relates to the collecting objectives of a museum or cultural institution (Cultural Heritage Agency, 2014; Reed, 2018; Russell & Winkworth, 2009). What is and is not significant is, of course, culturally and contextually specific, and shifts and changes with the coming and going of cultural norms and practices. With this in mind, this chapter will unpack the practice of significance as it relates to collecting social media, attempting to tease out which aspects of the practice we can apply to collecting social media, what needs to be reassessed or reviewed and what else needs to be considered in order for museums and those who work in them to understand the significance of social media content and objects. The first aspect is to understand the similarities and differences between physical and digital objects.

DOI: 10.4324/9781032669656-3

How do born-digital objects differ from physical objects?

How exactly has the digital world reconfigured how we understand museum objects, their interpretive role within a museum and the collecting practices of museums? The answer to this question is constantly changing with new technological advances. However, the value of comparing physical objects to digital objects can help to identify how collecting and interpretive practices have and haven't changed because of digital and internet technologies, including social media. Doing so can isolate the kinds of social media objects that museums might collect from a very large and growing body of content.

Museum studies scholar Susan Pearce (1994) compellingly draws on Saussure to think through the ways individual objects acquire meaning in museums as collections and through display. Turning to an infantry officer's jacket at the National Army Museum in London, she discusses how meaning is made when the presentation of the object and its documented history come into conversation with other objects on display and visitors' own lived experiences and collective understandings of the world. The role of Lieutenant Henry Anderson in the 1815 Battle of Waterloo is brought to life by the red jacket displayed alongside a letter penned by Anderson referencing the bullet wound he received to his left shoulder. Using his military uniform as evidence, Pearce argues that objects collected and displayed by museums operate as symbols that function to put forward a particular social and historical context. In the case of Henry Anderson, the Battle of Waterloo is made real via the jacket, which is ripped and marked with blood. Pearce explains that by selecting and presenting objects in such a way, museums construct meaning to expand a viewer's understanding of a person, place and event. In this case, the jacket is displayed with the letter and other objects of significance, carefully sourced and presented to create an imaginary understanding of this historic battle and Anderson's role in it. The jacket is used as a tool to help visitors bridge the past and the present. It helps to make tangible the physical impact of the war by presenting a personal account along with an emotional insight into a well-known historical moment.

Similarly, social media objects are selected by curators to construct meaning for audiences, especially in relation to how history and culture play out online. A historic event (a referendum), an issue of significance (climate change) or a popular online trend (the ice bucket challenge) are all examples of social media objects that a museum might collect and display to say something about contemporary culture. The Museum of London (MoL), a leader in the space of social media collecting, acquired 13 social media objects from the platform formerly known as Twitter, created during a 2020 COVID-19 lockdown, in order to document the experiences of Londoners during this tumultuous time. MoL limited its collecting to posts that had gone viral, defined by being shared 30,000 times or more. In one of the social media objects collected, a user writes they ordered tampons from Amazon but instead were sent 'a bag of 50 frozen sausage rolls' as the 'closest appropriate thing' (Knott, 2021). The social media post (the object) demonstrates a 'humour and sarcasm [that] have always been an inherent characteristic of Londoners but especially employed as coping mechanisms throughout history in times of crisis and hardship' (Knott, 2021). Much like Henry Anderson's red military jacket, the social media object transports viewers/audiences to a time and a place to communicate an important historical moment (COVID-19 and the lockdowns) by presenting an individual story in context.

Despite the similarities of physical and social media objects when it comes to meaning-making and interpretive capacities, a significant challenge for museums when collecting social media is that the array of objects from which a curator might select seems infinite. The sheer volume of digital content being created online makes it challenging, if not overwhelming, to decide what and what not to collect for posterity. Compounding this, much of what a museum might collect from social media is housed across different media platforms and created without the intention of collection, with some platforms serving as streams of consciousness sites rather than locations for carefully considered content creation. The ways in which content is created and understood in real time mean users do not necessarily understand what they create as important to human experience and worthy of keeping and collecting in the long term. Given that social and cultural uptake of social media is approaching an estimated five billion people, Wong (2024) suggests that its ubiquitous use is driven in part by community expectations – a fear of missing out on everyday communications with friends, family and businesses. This contrasts with practice where individuals make active decisions to use and create content online, as perhaps they did in the early days of its emergence. Because of this normalising use, we have yet to see many people offering their social media archives to museums or other collecting institutions, at least without prompting by museums themselves. In order to change this, the curator's role in not only actively collecting social media but also in educating the public about the importance of everyday and seemingly unremarkable social media use as socially, culturally and historically important is vital and evolving. This is where practices of contemporary and rapid response collecting are instructive.

Contemporary and rapid response collecting

Like many objects, stories and histories that require an active approach to collecting, social media requires an active approach. Contemporary collecting is a mode of collecting 'history as it happens' or collecting the current moment. The scholarship associated with this approach to building cultural collections remains nascent, but important contributions that support and advocate for the practice include the scholarship of Message (2014), Rhys (2011) and Rhys and Baveystock (2014). Kylie Message (2014, p. 84), for example, articulates contemporary collecting as falling into four categories: Cause-based collecting; collecting from sites of trauma, terrorism, war and natural disasters; collecting elections and contemporary politics; and collecting everyday and popular consumer culture. She explains that museums collect material because 'it's rare or unique, because it's representative … [and/or] because it's part of a set' (p. 84), and this too informs their specific contemporary collecting practices. Owain Rhys (2011, p. 29) describes the practice of contemporary collecting as attempting to be 'objective, current and representative, using local voices and memories,' and highlights the curatorial workload implications compared with other forms of collecting. That which has been articulated in museum scholarship has focused on the collecting of physical artefacts that represent present-day events and occurrences that are of a high profile (crisis, protest, natural disaster, conflict and so on). In practice, museums have much longer histories of collecting contemporary objects and histories. However, as a defined practice, the scholarship only goes as far back as the early 2000s, covering the public roll-out of the internet. Yet digital materials/objects/artefacts and technologies have been given scant attention in discussions of contemporary collecting.

Rapid response collecting, as a specific mode of contemporary collecting, is orientated towards collecting physical and/or digital objects to document an account of important historical events as they unfold in real time. While many museums are concerned primarily with collecting physical artefacts, it is not only through tangible objects that culture is experienced and shared. Rapid response collecting can involve physical objects such as face masks or vaccines in response to a pandemic, but it also can encapsulate digital objects shared in online spaces – for example, Instagram reels presenting empty airport terminals. Therefore, a rapid-response approach to contemporary collecting involves monitoring constantly evolving spaces that comprise both the physical and digital. These are places where communities negotiate and express meaning in real time, reflected in authentic accounts of their lived experiences. Rapid response collecting in the museum might involve dispatching staff or implementing a process to collect artefacts on a specific topic of social interest.

Museum studies scholar Sandro Debono (2021) credits this form of collecting as originating from the September 11 terrorist attacks and the New York Historical Society's response. It is described as an approach that seeks out 'relevant materials during or immediately following major events like celebrations, protests, and natural disasters' (New York Historical Society, 2025). Since September 11, the History Responds program has not only collected material artefacts from the terrorist attacks but has also documented Black Lives Matter protests, Occupy Wall Street, the 2017 Women's Marches, March for Our Lives and the Climate Strike events, among many other significant social events. The Victoria and Albert (V&A) Museum has adopted a slightly different approach to rapid response collecting since 2014. It endeavours to acquire and display innovations in the design and manufacturing of the current day. The V&A describes their rapid response project as collecting contemporary objects

> in response to major moments in recent history that touch the world of design and manufacturing. Many of the objects have been newsworthy

> either because they advance what design can do, or because they reveal truths about how we live.
>
> (Victoria and Albert Museum, 2022a)

While uniquely different in its disciplinary focus, the tendency to collect in response to 'major moments in recent history' is common. A toolkit commissioned by Museum Development North West (MDNW) and Arts Council England articulates contemporary collecting in the context of museum collecting practices and presents a number of case studies (Kavanagh, 2019). Much of what is captured in this toolkit leans on traditional modes of collecting material culture, with born-digital material described as 'content that was made digitally such as digital photographs, oral history recordings or film' (Kavanagh, 2019, p. 16). The major focus of these examples is the collection of material artefacts, reaffirming an assumption that what museums collect is physical.

Contemporary and rapid response collecting asks tough questions of museums. Is what feels significant now going to be significant in the future? Do we collect more in the moment and rely on deaccessioning practices in the future to ensure we don't risk loss, but rather assess what is significant or not after some time has passed? If we don't collect and wait, what will we forget or lose? These questions and many more are important to consider, especially as they relate to internet cultures. Social media is constantly changing with every new update, platforms come and go in rapid succession, and accounts are altered, edited and deleted by users on a daily basis. This context and these questions signal to us that museums must improve by first acknowledging the importance of social media and its content and working through not only how to collect it from a technical perspective but also how to gauge its significance to ensure that, as much as we can, the right content is being collected for future generations. Determining what is the 'right content' from the perspective of the collecting remit of specific institutions is fraught. In the same way that they assess the significance of physical objects, museums must adopt a shared methodology for assessing significance as it relates to social media objects, so museum collections are not chaotic in nature but rather meaningful through the decisions that curators and others make to include, retain or reject objects and stories.

Born-digital collecting

Alongside the development of contemporary collecting practices, we find those of digitisation and born-digital collecting. This book does not seek to reiterate or further theorise digitisation as a museological practice. Instead, we are concerned with objects that are not copies, replicas, reproductions, surrogates and so on of physical collections, but those that are created firmly within digital systems and infrastructures. Born-digital collecting is a practice that aims to identify, collect, document and preserve objects born in the digital realm. It refers to 'digital works which are not copies of analogue documents' but instead 'exist only in the digital space' (Victorian Collections, 2021) and have never existed in any other context. Born-digital objects consist of 'photographs,' 'harvested web content,' 'digital documents,' 'digital manuscripts,' 'electronic records,' 'static data sets,' 'dynamic data,' 'digital art' and 'digital media publications' (Erway, 2010). This includes content streamed on services such as Netflix and Amazon Prime, as well as blogs, emails, websites and other forms of material distributed on social media. Conceived and distributed in a digital format and through digital platforms, these objects are often not considered in existing museum policy documents, which are largely orientated to the collection, documentation and preservation of physical objects. While we acknowledge the wide and diverse range of born-digital objects, we are focused specifically on what Gabi Arrigoni (2022), research fellow at the Victoria and Albert Museum, refers to as 'big tech heritage' – that is, social media content housed on privately owned media platforms. Specifically, this references the everyday content generated by users of social media that is subsequently shared on social media platforms.

It is important to acknowledge that for the past 30 years or more, archives and libraries have been working on strategies to collect and preserve born-digital content (Waters & Garrett, 1996). In terms of industry-based resources on digital collecting, the OCLC (2024) has created a suite of useful reports that include (among others) *Defining Born Digital* and *Born Digital* (video), which articulate precisely what these objects are. Another, *Walk This Way: Detailed Steps for Transferring Born-digital Content from Media You Can Read In-house*, provides guidance on how to access key tools and resources, and *The Archival Advantage: Integrating Archival Expertise into Management of Born-digital Library Materials* presents important principles and techniques. The focus of the library and archive sector has largely been on preserving rather than on curation. The Internet Archive, for example, which was formed in 1996, makes copies of digital content so it might be made available later. The Smithsonian Institution Archives (SMA) helpfully differentiates between digital preservation and digital curation. Digital preservation is described as 'the task of ensuring that digital collections are accessible to the public in the future,' whereas 'digital curation encompasses the selection, acquisition, preservation, maintenance, and delivery of digital data' (Smithsonian Institution Archives, 2025). This is helpful for museums, which are focused on curating collections as opposed to seeking to collect and preserve everything comprehensively.

In recognising the work of libraries and archives, we are not suggesting that digital objects have never been collected by museums – in fact, the opposite is true, and many museums have engaged in collecting photography, film, sound, video games and more. However, there is a lack of agreed-upon strategies and processes for their collection and curation (Zuanni, 2021), in strong contrast to the agreed practices for physical objects. The Victoria and Albert Museum (V&A) has produced three particularly important reports through an Arts and Humanities Research Council project titled Preserving and Sharing Born Digital and Hybrid Objects. The project addresses the challenges of preserving, collecting and meaningfully sharing born-digital and hybrid digital objects in museum collections, focusing on three interrelated but separate areas: Collection management, digital preservation and public access. The first report, titled *Preserving and Sharing Born-Digital and Hybrid Objects from Across the National Collection Report* (Victoria and Albert Museum, 2022b), raises challenges associated with cataloguing, preserving and providing access to born-digital and hybrid objects. The second, a Decision Model Report also titled *Preserving and Sharing Born-Digital and Hybrid Objects from Across the National Collection Report* (Victoria and Albert Museum, 2022c) presents a number of flow charts as tools designed to help professionals navigate decision-making as it relates to collecting and digital preservation of born-digital and hybrid museum objects. The third, a data modelling for born-digital/hybrid objects report titled *Born Digital, Born Slippery* (Victoria and Albert Museum, 2022d), looks closely at the issues related to cataloguing born-digital and hybrid objects within existing cataloguing standards to determine whether and how they can be supported. Notably, these reports contribute to our understanding of the complexities of social media artefacts, especially from a technical and collection management perspective. The first report produced ten key recommendations for future work in this space. In the context of our current contribution, recommendations two and three identify a requirement for an expanded role of the curator in the space of born-digital collecting and the need for models that articulate the value of this type of collecting.

A growing number of bodies support museums with digital preservation, and through their work, they have produced reports and guidance on born-digital collecting. The Australian Emulation Network, for example, is designed to provide researchers and gallery, library, archive and museum (GLAM) professionals working with born-digital artefacts with an infrastructure and community of practice. However, it is largely centred on media arts, design and architecture and does not focus specifically on social media collecting (Swalwell, 2022). Despite this, the Australian Emulation Network does encompass some social media objects within its collection, and the findings of the project are likely to help guide future work in this space. The Digital Preservation Coalition similarly has long been working in this space and in 2015 produced a handbook (Digital Preservation Coalition, 2015) that provides helpful guidance on born-digital collecting. While it should be viewed as an early publication, it highlights enduring challenges to the sector, such as data loss and storage.

What the existing literature and practice make clear is that by their very nature, born-digital objects are difficult for museums to collect because they are reliant upon digital infrastructures (often privately owned) for their storage and distribution (Arrigoni & McKim, 2022). Alongside the technical challenges – which, for many museums, are paralysing – there is a seemingly limited acknowledgement that such material is worthy of collection by museums. Even when museums acknowledge the social, cultural and historical value of social media, there are often challenges in determining what to collect among the large and growing body of content being produced online. We believe that social media asks new and different questions of significance, and as such, the practice of significance in the context of museums requires attention and review to support this kind of collecting.

The practice of significance

Significance as a museological practice is the process of identifying and assessing an object's meaning to establish its significance to a group of people, a place, a topic and a particular museum collection. Significance is not fixed in time and is impacted by changes in communities, cultures, politics, science and the environment over time and in relation to other objects, events and ideas. Perhaps the most important Australian publication on the topic is *Significance 2.0*, written by Roslyn Russell and Kylie Winkworth (2009) and published by the Collections Council of Australia, a national collections sector industry council that was set up and supported by the Cultural Ministers Council of Australia from 2004 to 2010. *Significance 2.0* is currently under review by the Australian Government's Office for the Arts, and it is anticipated that this review will consider digital cultural material in greater depth. The publication, as it stands in 2025, steps out the process by which museums and collecting institutions identify and assess significance. For many practitioners, the practice of significance will be second nature; however, to unpack significance in the context of social media objects, we believe it is important to return to basics and outline the practice here in order to identify the ways social media objects are asking new questions of significance and how this might impact curators and others responsible for building cultural collections.

Significance 2.0 outlines four categories of significance with which objects in museum collections are strongly associated (Russell & Winkworth, 2009, p. 39):

- *Historic significance:* A person, group, place or event that contributes to an understanding of events, people and developments in the past
- *Artistic or aesthetic significance*: Art and design, craft and the decorative arts contribute to an understanding of an artist, artistic movements, style and design
- *Scientific or research significance:* Scientific value across all disciplines and the incorporation of objects with potential research value, including archives, natural history or archaeological collections
- *Social or spiritual significance:* A particular, identified group of people or community that demonstrates a strong contemporary attachment between the objects and a group of people

In addition to these four categorisations of significance, *Significance 2.0* identifies comparative criteria (Russell & Winkworth, 2009, pp. 39–40), which can be applied to further evaluate significance; however, as the authors suggest, they should not be the only way significance is determined. These are:

- *Provenance:* The history of an object's ownership; it relates to the context of an object's use from its creation to the point it is acquired by a museum
- *Rarity:* Relates to uncommon or one-of-a-kind objects that speak to any area of significance
- *Representativeness:* Relates to objects that represent a group of people, a way of life or a theme that speaks to any area of significance
- *Condition or completeness:* Refers to the physicality of objects and how their physical condition contributes to their meaning
- *Interpretive capacity:* An object's ability to communicate themes, people or ideas relative to any area of significance

Significance 2.0 is an important publication for museum practitioners, especially in Australia. However, it was developed at a time when the objects of the internet were not being considered by museums in the same way as the material culture being produced. Therefore, the publication does not deal well with born-digital and social media objects. Far from this being a criticism of *Significance 2.0*, it signals the time required to understand new and emerging technologies and their implications on human societies. Sufficient time has passed to revisit the role of social media in society. Even with rapid changes to the platforms of the day, the fundamental idea that underpins social media is here to stay and thus deserves consideration in the context of significance.

The significance of digital things

To reiterate, the museum sector is grappling with what digital objects are and how to collect them. More than this, as humans, we are grappling with what we understand to be important when it comes to digital cultural output. Gabbi Arrigoni (2021) on the V&A blog says that 'born digital objects often do not "fit" the established instructional collections policies, information architectures, and intellectual property regimes which often determine what and how we collect.' While acknowledging the complexity of collecting born-digital material in the context of bits and networks, Arrigoni (2021) explains that the challenges of collecting born-digital material relate to cultures of 'participation, sharing and remix, that bring about questions of privacy, ownership, crediting and managing expectations.' Using an example that communicates a common experience of many social media users during the COVID-19 lockdowns – walking around, taking photos with their phones and sharing them on social media – Chiara Zuanni (2021, p. 188) describes how the social media post consists of 'the author (myself), the instrument (my smartphone), and the object (the graffiti) that inspired the photograph and its short accompanying text.' Zuanni's point is that social media objects are not only made up of their visual and textual elements – those a user might see – but also incorporate elements that may or may not be important to how the object is understood and collected. She uses the term 'assemblage' to explain this complexity that defines social media objects. Furthermore, social media platforms compress and resize images and other media (such as photos taken with a smartphone and uploaded) to ensure there is enough bandwidth for their websites to load and deliver content to users quickly, compromising the quality of the original. If another user downloads and re-shares that image, it will be compressed and resized again, further reducing the quality. This brings into question traditional notions of authenticity and provenance, and museums are becoming increasingly comfortable with the potential of multiple owners and donors. Fiona Cameron (2021, p. 5) explains that digital cultural heritage is not only a 'reflection of human creativity mediated through data and technical systems but also encompasses the creative impulses of a wide range of other-than-human actors' – for instance, artificial intelligence (AI). So, while museums grapple with the complex significance and provenance of internet cultures, including social media, they must also be cognisant of what is being produced by humans and what is increasingly not, and how that informs collecting. Enhanced knowledge about the logics of social media, at least in its current form, can assist museums in better understanding context and how the logics of social media might play into how we understand social media objects and their meanings.

The logics of social media

In addressing the significance of social media, museums and their professionals must pay attention to its logics. We can no longer rely solely on the logics of the material world to identify and assess the significance of things that exist and are produced in the digital realm, especially on social media. José van Dijck and Thomas Poell (2013) helpfully articulate four key logics of social media – programmability, popularity, connectivity and datafication – all of which impact multiple areas of public life, including news and broadcasting, law and order, social activism and change, politics and more. Van Dijck and Poell's social media logics can assist museums in understanding the interplay of such logics with society and thus support an expanded understanding of significance in museums, especially as it relates to the objects of social media. So, how are the four key logics of social media defined, and what can museums learn from them?

The first logic of social media is programmability, defined as the ability of social media platforms to trigger and steer users' creative or communicative contributions, while users, through their interaction with coded social media environments, may in turn influence such a platform (van Dijck & Poell, 2013). Technologically, programmability is underpinned by computer code, data, algorithms, protocols, interfaces and the platform organisations that are responsible for programming. Through coded instructions, platforms shape relational activities, such as liking, recommending, sharing and so on.

Programmability also relates to human agency, which individuals enact through their own contributions to the platforms or when they resist coded instructions or defy protocols (van Dijck & Poell, 2013). When this happens, platforms may change their approach and reprogram their algorithms to meet the needs of their users. In short, programmability represents a relationship between the human and coded aspects of the social media ecosystem. Programmability influences what every user sees and engages with, and thus it requires critical attention from a museum perspective. The way social media is experienced by a creator is not necessarily the same as how another user will experience it, so the context in which engagement takes place is important to document. Museums must recognise the bias inherent in social media algorithmic logics to ensure that when collecting social media, the perspectives of the user or creator are well documented. This, in turn, offers some safeguard that objects of social media are understood in a way that will not suggest in the future that every iteration of contemporary social media platforms is the same or experienced in the same way.

The logic of popularity (van Dijck & Poell, 2013) refers to the techniques that social media platforms use to filter out popular items and influential people. Popularity as a social media logic is informed by platform algorithms and socioeconomics. Popularity manifests through likes, comments, views and so on, resulting in platforms identifying trending topics based on engagement data. While the logic of popularity is not new, social media adds a layer of complexity due to the human agency of users and creators, who can influence trending topics and popularise content by actively participating in likes, shares and comments to push forward content (van Dijck & Poell, 2013). Virality intersects with popularity and can often influence views of how important or significant a social media object is. Museums must remain attentive to the role of users and creators in creating popularity on social media platforms and assess the significance of social media objects within this context. Popularity – or virality, for that matter – may not represent other spheres of social and cultural life. This is not a bad thing, nor does it suggest that what happens on social media is not authentic or valid, but that museums must pay attention to the context in which popularity manifests on social media. Popularity can fluctuate across platforms, as each social media domain will approach popularity in varying ways, and so what plays out on one social media platform may not on another because of differing demographics and sociocultural backgrounds of their user cohorts.

The third logic of social media is connectivity, which underscores how social media emerged from a very human desire to communicate and connect (van Dijck & Poell, 2013). At a rapid rate, social media platforms have evolved from relatively simple user-to-user information exchange to virtual sites of gathering and connection. People buy, swap and sell in a retail sense, host public and private meetings and establish meaningful relationships online through social media. Van Dijck and Poell (2013) explain that the intention of social media to promote, even create, human connection is still part of social media logic;

however, they suggest the term 'connectivity' to better articulate the nuance of how it plays out online. Connectivity 'refers to the socio-technical affordance of networked platforms to connect content to user activities and advertisers' (van Dijck & Poell, 2013, p. 8). This means that the platform – or more specifically its coded ecosystem – mediates the activities of users and defines how connectivity occurs. It manifests clearly through recommendation culture on social media platforms – that is, how platforms use algorithms to understand user behaviour and then recommend content to users. As van Dijck and Poell (2013, p. 9) explain, recommendations on social media connect 'users to content, users to users, platforms to users, users to advertisers, and platforms to platforms.' There is nothing inherently wrong with this, but within a museum context, understanding how technological intervention directs human connection and connectedness will impact how we understand the significance of social media objects.

The fourth and final logic of social media, as defined by van Dijck and Poell (2013), is datafication, which is the phenomenon of quantification of human experience through data or digital information. Within a social media context, this refers to a networked platform's ability to quantify data that has never been quantified before – more than demographics, in an online setting, it includes images and videos, music and books, and in a social media setting, it includes likes, comments, trends and interpersonal relationships (van Dijck & Poell, 2013). Ultimately, everything is data that can be used to understand people and what they want based on the choices they make. Data and its use are not new – nations collect census data on their citizens to influence policy and programmes, and for decades, television and radio have collected viewership data to determine future programming. What makes datafication in the social media space different is that it can and does happen instantaneously, and while users have agency through likes, comments, shares and so on, datafication can also drive users to view and engage with certain content, make purchases or make new friends. This notion of datafication and how it is employed in a social media setting is important for museums to understand, especially in order to recognise how people are using and being used by platforms, and what that means when it comes to reflections of social media use and meaning applied by users to their content and social media objects. This is not to suggest that social media experiences are inauthentic, but that there are many factors influencing how users engage, and that individual engagement is driven by datafication and therefore won't necessarily be the same as other engagements.

There are, of course, many other facets to social media that inform its logics – and indeed, for the technologically minded, there is software, code, algorithms and more to think through to understand the complexity of platforms. We are not technical experts, nor do we expect those working in museums and other cultural institutions to be. For us, understanding social media logic is about context and how that context emerges in what museums determine is significant to a group of people, a place or a topic. What the logics of social media offer to the museum sector is a more nuanced picture of social media, highlighting the need to critically engage with social media objects from a different perspective than we might when engaging with tangible material culture.

Implications for significance assessments

Understanding the logics of social media is important for museums if we acknowledge the importance of the object type. Bram and Titia van der Werf (2020, p. 175) suggest that 'traditional models for selecting and preserving cultural heritage no longer apply.' Having outlined the established practice of significance in museums – the logics that underpin how museums decide what is and is not significant to their own missions – and unpacked some of the key principles that underpin the logics of social media, we can start to see where social media objects require museums to ask further questions and consider different things as they relate to the unique contexts and ecosystems of social media. To appreciate the complexity of social media objects, we have identified some social media objects currently housed on social media platforms and produced significance assessments for them. None of these examples, to our knowledge, have been collected by museums or other cultural institutions, yet each provides insights into the complexity of social media objects. Our intention is for these examples to highlight questions and considerations that social media objects pose to those developing cultural collections.

The democracy sausage

A sausage with tomato sauce on a slice of white bread, irreverently known as a 'democracy sausage,' is sold at community fundraising stalls hosted at Australian election polling places. In recent years, the democracy sausage has become a symbol of Australian democratic traditions, alongside pioneering innovations including the secret ballot, universal suffrage and compulsory voting. It serves as an extension of the 'sausage sizzle' – a distinctly Australian community-orientated spin on the barbecue. It references Australia's larrikin culture and works to unite people irrespective of personal political preferences during the conduct of elections, and always in support of charitable causes. As a playful symbol of a national community, it is no surprise that the democracy sausage found its way onto social media.

Emojis of democracy sausages have enabled Australians to engage with the uniquely Australian tradition online. The democracy sausage emoji (the object) has been released periodically by the social media platform formerly known as Twitter and appears to have first been made available as a temporary emoji for those tweeting the #ausvotes hashtag during the 2016 Australian federal election (Ewbank, 2017). Twitter subsequently offered the democracy sausage emoji to users in the 2019 and 2022 federal elections, also as a temporary emoji associated with election-related hashtags. During the 2022

Australian election campaign, this included #sausagesizzle, #AusVotes2022, #DemocracySausage, #AusVotes, #AusPol, and #MyFirstDemocracySausage (X Australia, 2022).

There is no doubt in the minds of these Australian authors that the democracy sausage is culturally significant to Australian society and democracy. The application of the symbol within a social media environment is increasingly important as democracy, in general, plays out online in a twenty-first-century context. Looking at *Significance 2.0* (Russell & Winkworth, 2009), we can articulate the significance of the democracy sausage emoji within the category of social and cultural significance. Its significance is embodied through its referencing of the tradition of the election-day sausage sizzle, events that take place at polling places (such as public schools and community halls) across the country to bring people together and raise funds for charitable causes – a representation of Australia's democratic ideals.

As discussed earlier, the concept of significance for social media objects has much overlap with physical objects. However, the democracy sausage emoji offers a clear point of difference and raises new questions that impact its significance assessment. The first is the impermanence of the emoji as represented on the social media platform formally known as Twitter. As a temporary feature made available to users employing specific hashtags, and for a period that is defined and controlled by the platform, the democracy sausage emoji's sporadic existence generally aligns with that of its tangible culinary inspiration during Australia's federal and state election campaigns. Even the platform's own tweet announcing the return of the democracy sausage emoji for the 2022 Australian federal election excludes the emoji when viewed outside of the period for which the emoji is enabled (X Australia, 2022). This brings into question when and how museums should collect objects that include the democracy sausage emoji. Given the impermanence of the emoji, collecting it after its period of use poses risks to the object's authenticity – for example, the code and design that created the emoji and the visual environment of the platform will likely change at each election, so curators and collection managers must ask whether the design of the emoji and its relationship with the specific context of the election and/or the social media platform at the time of its posting are important to the significance and authenticity of the object.

Another consideration to which the democracy sausage emoji alerts us is the operating systems used by users posting and receiving information through social media. Users tweeting via different devices (e.g., Apple or Samsung) and operating systems (iOS or Android) will be offered different versions of the democracy sausage emoji. Because of this, tweets appear to be somewhat agnostic in terms of operating system, meaning that unless a tweet (or component such as an emoji) is captured and collected in a static form, the emoji may change in appearance when accessed in different operating system environments. Therefore, museums and their curators must identify whether the visual characteristics of the social media object are important to its significance, and if so, this will impact the decisions about how and from what sources the emoji is collected.

Inuit representation

As social media has emerged as a key mode of communication, so has its role in shaping cultural practices. Shina Novalinga, also known as Shina Nova, identifies as an Inuit woman. She gained notoriety on TikTok and Instagram for posting videos of herself and her mother throat singing, a cultural practice of Inuit communities; they have attracted four million followers on TikTok. Novalinga explores aspects of her cultural heritage on social media to educate her audience about Inuit cultural practices, including language, tattooing, food sources such as whale meat and North American Indigenous histories. Her social media content can be considered a mode of cultural preservation as well as education, offering insights into Inuit culture, traditions and practices. The historical significance of Novalinga's work is especially important because Inuit throat singing was banned by Christian missionaries in the early twentieth century, leading to its near-extinction (Balsam & Foden, 2021; Black, 2018). The practice was revived in the 1980s, and Shina's mother learnt it from Puvirnituq elders and taught it to her daughter (Nath, 2021; Young & McMahon, 2021). Using contemporary social media tools, Novalinga is passing down knowledge and culture to a wide audience.

Indigenous cultures have been ignored or misrepresented in mainstream media, whereas Novalinga's videos offer an unfiltered, first-hand account of Inuit life (Allaire, 2020). Her creative endeavours align with broader cultural revitalisation movements to preserve Indigenous languages and traditions. They not only educate non-Indigenous audiences but also inspire young Indigenous people to embrace their heritage (Nath, 2021; Young & McMahon, 2021). Novalinga's contributions extend beyond entertainment and education, as she addresses serious social issues such as the crisis of missing and murdered Indigenous women in Canada (Young & McMahon, 2021), demonstrating how social media can be a tool for advocacy and social change.

Intangible cultural heritage, such as songs, music, dances, drama, skills, food, sports, crafts and festivals, is something that museums have historically struggled to collect – dancing is often represented by costumes, music via instruments and cooking with utensils. However, there is an argument that what is significant about such cultural practices is the intangible – the dance, the choreography, the sounds and lights and the smells and tastes. Social media provides new opportunities to collect contemporary intangible cultural heritage by virtue of its format – that is, the bringing together of screen-based visual and audio elements. Firmly part of the communication and preservation of intangible cultural heritage, social media offers museums a new, more meaningful way to collect such cultural heritage.

'I am flaming gay'

Indonesians who identify as having diverse sexuality and gender experience social, religious, economic, political and legal discrimination (Triastuti, 2021). As a result of ongoing discrimination, many lesbian, gay, bisexual, transgender, intersex and queer + (LGBTIQ+) Indonesians have embraced social media as a space to express themselves, document their experiences and share their stories (Triastuti, 2021). Alongside this, LGBTIQ+ activists use social media to deploy their ideas and messages to a captive audience. Lesbian singer-songwriter Kai Mata is one such activist. On 28 February 2020, in response to a bill proposed to the Indonesian Parliament known as the Family Resilience Bill – which would require citizens with 'deviant' sexual persuasions to undergo 'rehabilitation' (Walden & Souisa, 2020) – Mata made a post to multiple social media platforms, including Instagram and Twitter (now X), in which she uses video, music and text to advocate against the proposed law. She says, 'My name is Kai Mata. I am Indonesian and I am also flaming gay. No laws will change that, no conversion therapy will change that, and neither will the hate and threats' (Mata, 2020). This was Mata's first viral moment on social media (Renaldi, 2024), and that post on Twitter (now X) has 15,000 likes and 9500 shares, and her Instagram post has 6440 views. The posts received positive and negative responses in the form of comments and re-shares. In response to the commentary on Twitter, Mata commented on her own posts, saying that 'for every one message rooted in ignorance, there are 10 rooted in support and love. I promise you change is happening' (Mata, 2020). Mata represents a younger generation of Indonesians who identify as having diverse sexuality and/or who are increasingly dissatisfied with their country's laws and social attitudes towards queer people and engaged in activism on social media. Online activism by LGBTIQ+ Indonesians, and especially young people, is significant to Indonesian social and cultural histories associated with LGBTIQ+ experience. This is happening globally, with LGBTIQ+ youth utilising social media as a form of active resistance to improve their well-being by creating distance from their stressed lived experiences and gaining a sense of control over their lives (Craig et al., 2015).

In our analysis, it is unclear, but probably Kai Mata created and edited her video outside of the social media platforms and posted it to multiple platforms. In this case, does the platform matter? The post gained more attention on Twitter and likely had a bigger impact, which is not surprising given its more public context and use for news and other communications. The virality of the posts speaks to the significance of the issues, the public profile of the creator and the impact of the messaging on those who received it. This example demonstrates that the 'authenticity' of a social media object does not necessarily reside in the creation of the video – likely filmed on a smartphone and edited in other applications before being posted online. The 'authenticity' of Mata's post rests in social media, inclusive of the engagements that occurred in response to the original post. Therefore, we can argue that because of the impact of the post on Twitter, we might decide to collect that iteration of the post.

Another factor relating to 'authenticity' is the look and feel of the web-based environment in which the post was published by the creator. In 2020, when Mata posted her video, the platform known as Twitter was graphically different from the platform now known as X, fully rebranded from its past identity. Mata's content still exists on the new platform but has been altered by the rebrand. This asks museums to consider whether the graphic elements of the social media object are important and, if so, whether museums might consider taking a rapid-response approach to collecting the content. This is no longer an option, so we must consider the changing nature of social media as part of the object's history. Social media platforms are constantly updated from a visual and technical perspective, and if this is accepted and documented, the notion of authenticity is shown to be malleable in the context of collecting social media.

Finally, the virality of Mata's post speaks to impact, and therefore, curatorially, we might decide to capture comments and reshares as part of the object to express that aspect of the object's story. We might decide that we want to capture every comment and reshare, or some representative examples of them. Either option is a valid choice that must be considered by the curator from a curatorial perspective and in the context of organisational capacities. This is where the curator's role expands – a social media object, unlike a physical object, is ultimately re-created by those capturing it, depending on the approach taken to collect, store and preserve it. Screenshots, web recordings and emulation are examples of capturing online content that museums and other institutions collect. Collecting in this way ultimately creates a copy of the digital-born object that may still exist in other online settings. Museums must accept that the nature of social media objects is different from physical objects and that copies created through digital preservation activities are authentic objects in their own right. The collection, control and care of a social media object requires museums to accept that the existence of other versions of it will be in circulation and, in the case of social media, live online.

These three examples represent social media objects live online at the time of writing. To our knowledge, none of these examples have been collected or even considered for collection by a museum or any other institution. What they represent are examples of social media that have value for museums and their missions. The examples provide a lens to develop an understanding of the significance of social media objects and the social and cultural import of social media in society. They articulate the contexts in which social media objects exist and their differences from physical objects that point to ways to find value in such objects and their role in museum collections, both now and into the future. While not a comprehensive outline of all possible impacts with regard to significance within a social media context, these examples confirm that approaches to determining the significance of museum collections must change with new and emerging object types.

Provenance and authenticity

Before we go on, we must acknowledge that in an age of fake social media accounts, which impersonate real people and spread false information, there is a need for the museum to ascertain the origin and authenticity of a digital object or risk damaging its credibility as a collecting institution. There are now more opportunities than ever for digital content to be manipulated and falsified, further driving the need for codes of practice that limit image manipulation (Bushey, 2016). Museums, like news media, have established standards that are designed to ensure that objects are authentic before they are acquired. However, given the nature of social media, it becomes increasingly difficult to fact-check a digital object's provenance, with the notable exception of non-fungible tokens (NFTs) that use blockchain technology to track ownership. As Jessica Bushey (2016, p. 17) rightfully points out, 'if we want the assurance of the trustworthiness of a photograph, we need to verify that the photograph is capable of standing in for the facts to which it asserts.' This means that, when collecting social media content, museums should endeavour, when possible, to collect associated metadata that helps to identify its trustworthiness. While different platforms vary in terms of how much metadata they retain, it can include important contextual information such as the date when a file was created, the location, the name of the person who posted it and the place where it was created and uploaded. This can be tricky, as some social platforms can be more helpful than others in terms of identifying who created what. For example, on TikTok, 'Please Credit Videos' is a way in which authors seek acknowledgement of their content, ranging from dance moves to trends (Abidin, 2021). However, there is a lot of fakery, making it especially important to check its provenance using other means. This includes acquiring the permission of the user and researching provenance through interviews with the creator to understand, for example, whether any element of the social media object was created using a third-party platform or taken offline using a smartphone or other device. By asking the right questions, curators can determine where ownership lies.

New considerations for social media significance

In this section, we discuss some of the key considerations that museums must address, as they apply to social media objects, when undertaking significance assessments. These considerations pose new questions for museums and will be useful in the long term, noting that as technology changes, more questions and considerations will need to be thought through. The following is intended to support curators and those developing cultural collections to determine significance beyond content and context and to consider specific issues relevant to social media.

Online environments

When thinking about social media, we must contemplate the infrastructure that facilitates human engagement in online spaces. When assessing the significance of social media objects, we must ask whether the online environment is important to the significance of the object. Does the design or functionality of the online environment provide insights into why something is significant? If a social media object is not being collected in real time, then has the platform design and functionality changed since the object's original posting, and do any changes impact the authenticity or significance of the object?

Sociality

Social media, as its name articulates, is inherently social, so human connection continues to be a driver for social media platforms. The social aspect of social media is what differentiates it from other forms of digital content creation. Therefore, when assessing the significance of social media objects, we must ask whether the reactions, comments, likes or shares are important to the story. Have any reactions been deleted or hidden from view, and does that impact the significance of the object or the way it should be documented? Do we need to collect or capture all reactions, or will a representative selection work to support the significance of a social media object?

Relationality

Social media does not exist in isolation, and what is produced in those spaces is often a response to someone's material world and other life experiences. So, we must ask whether the social media object is in reaction to an event or moment that has occurred offline or outside the social media environment. For example, is it about a natural disaster, a political statement or a specific event? Is that moment or occurrence part of the object's significance? Is it possible to communicate the object's significance without the contextual linkages? How can the context in which the social media object was created be carefully or exhaustively documented to ensure long-term understanding of its origin and impact?

Platforms

There are many social media platforms, and they will continue to emerge, disappear or morph as technological advances are made. Individuals often use multiple platforms and post the same or similar content to a variety of competing platforms. When assessing the significance of social media objects, we must ask whether the digital object was posted to a single site or to many platforms. Do we need to collect instances of the object being published on different platforms? Is the platform irrelevant to its significance, and would collecting the files uploaded to social media be more useful? How should its use on social media be documented, if not by collecting the online environment?

Users as creators

Users are creators who conceive, produce and publish content online for their connections, friends, families and audiences. This means we should consider the intention of the user or creator in understanding the significance of social media objects. Therefore, we must ask whether the user's intention behind posting is part of the object's significance and how that will be documented. Will users have a say in the way the object is interpreted? Will this be done in the same way that creative practitioners and artists determine how their work is shown?

Human and non-human actors

Contemporary social media includes accounts and content created and communicated by AI and synthetic media. While there is nothing wrong with this, it is important for curators and those building cultural collections to be aware of such content and accounts and to document how human and non-human interaction happens online, especially when it relates to social media objects identified for collection.

Display and interpretation

Something with which museums are grappling is how to display born-digital objects. Should content created on a smartphone be displayed on a smartphone, or can museums extract files and project them on large surfaces? Perhaps a user or creator interview will provide guidance to determine the preferred form of display. When assessing the significance of a social media object, a secondary consideration is about display and interpretation. We must ask how the object could or should be displayed. Will additional code be required to represent the object in the future in a live environment, or will a copy/representation/emulation of the object be sufficient?

There are other things for museums to consider when collecting social media, such as technical capacity, storage, long-term preservation and costs. These are important considerations; however, our focus here has been to unpack the curatorial assessment of social media objects. The above considerations will assist cultural practitioners to not only determine what social media is important to their museum or collection but to drill down further regarding what specific aspects of that social media object hold particular meaning within the context of its publication. It should therefore be a focus of capture and collection. In doing this, we want to assert the need for robust curatorial assessment before technical assessment – or at least at the same time. All too often, the technical limitations of collecting social media overshadow the curatorial remit of the museum – yet, if museums are to meet their civic obligations, an understanding of what social media is significant to their collections, and particularly the elements that make it significant, will assist institutions to find the most appropriate technical solutions to collect it.

Conclusion

In this chapter, we have considered the difference between physical and digital objects, especially through the lens of significance. The museological practice of significance has undoubtedly been impacted by the internet and its digital objects, including social media. Specifically, new object types, like social media, have emerged and challenge the ways museums and their professionals determine what is and is not significant (or relevant) to collections. It is therefore imperative that museums and those building cultural collections update their approaches to significance assessments, especially for social media objects. This involves responding to new questions and considerations that have emerged with the new object type. These include considering the online environment, sociality, relationality, platforms, users as creators, human and non-human actors, and display and interpretation. In articulating these new considerations, we have argued that significance should be prioritised before the technical assessment of collecting digital and social media objects. This is to ensure that decisions taken to collect, or not, are informed by the cultural, social and historical significance of the object – again, as it would be with any physical artefact under consideration by a museum. This is not to say that technical considerations are not important, but they should not alone lead decision-making. By reviewing and reshaping significance assessments, museums will be better prepared to collect social media, not only from a content perspective but also to determine the technological requirements to do so.

Insights from practitioners

Foteini Aravani

> I think that museums are very good at finding one million reasons for not doing something, and copyright is always the number one. I was happy to take a risk which I felt was low, because otherwise we wouldn't be able to do anything.

Foteini Aravani, former Curator of Digital Collections and Oral Histories at the Museum of London (MoL), discussed with us how the MoL approached collecting social media in 2012 to document the London Olympics and in 2020 to document Londoners' experiences of the COVID-19 pandemic. Both projects differed in terms of approach: One through an open call for participation and one more targeted at collecting from specific accounts.

Just collect!

Foteini explained that museums must challenge their assumptions when engaging with digital cultural heritage objects. Simply stated, the inclusion of digital objects in a museum collection can fundamentally shift how museums regard objects in general. The more museums collect social media, the more they will understand it and value it, and their collection policies and decisions will evolve to better support the practice of collecting it. So, get collecting!

Working with platforms

Obtaining consent from users and navigating copyright issues can be a significant challenge to collecting social media. This includes copyright associated with platform design and branding. It is therefore important for museums to work closely with social media platforms to ensure compliance with the specific terms and conditions. Foteini explained that understanding a collection's intended use – commercial or non-commercial – will support museums to undertake this work. Museums, she said, should aim to build collaborative relationships with platforms to ensure the preservation of the important digital cultural heritage that exists on social media.

The changing nature of display

Foteini explained to us that audience feedback has played a crucial role in determining how the MoL has gone about displaying social media objects. Various methods were proposed to display the tweets (social media posts from the platform formerly known as Twitter) the museum had collected, including data visualisations and physical prints. In this instance, visitors preferred digital content displayed in physical frames. While this is not a direction for professionals, the decision of the MoL to include its audiences in display decisions demonstrates that audiences require education about digital objects and exposure to display approaches because they are so familiar with engaging with physical objects in museum spaces.

Kajsa Hartig

> We still have this issue that people don't see their stories [social media] as significant, even though we actually tell them, please we want you to tell us and share these fantastic stories.

Kajsa Hartig is Head of Culture at Kulturchef, Avesta kommun. Previously, she was Head of Museum Experience at Västernorrlands Museum in Sweden. Kajsa has collaborated with Scandinavian museums and digital infrastructure companies to develop platforms such as Minnen and Connect to Collect, a system for collecting digital cultural heritage.

Public participation and engagement

The public's willingness to contribute to social media collecting efforts has declined over time due to privacy concerns, digital fatigue and a lack of incentives to contribute content. Building trust and meaningful relationships is time-consuming but essential to collecting approaches, especially when working with marginalised communities. It is also important to give people options that will allow them to choose to publish their social media content publicly for everyone else to see, as well as to just archive it.

A complex legal and ethical landscape

A range of issues exists around General Data Protection Regulation (GDPR), consent and licensing that can present major barriers to collecting social media. This poses a challenge for museums, she explained, as they must navigate grey areas in data handling and ensure contributors understand how their content will be used and shared both now and in the future.

Curators as community facilitators

Curators are not just collectors and archivists but also community managers in that they shape collecting narratives and play a critical role in engaging contributors and (ideally) fostering ongoing dialogue using digital platforms.

The right infrastructure

When museums decide to collect social media through an online submission platform, Kajsa said, they need to seek out stable, user-friendly systems with the ability to sustain long-term digital collecting. The benefit of purpose-built systems for this type of collecting should not be under-estimated, and it supports institutions to ensure that processes around permissions and file formats can be standardised, reducing the risk of future use and loss.

Jason Scott

> To me there is an important social contract that never transferred to the internet. [It's like] we're gonna host your most precious memories, your work, and everything [else], and we have no contingency, none for getting rid of it beyond deleting you.

Jason Scott, Software Curator and Free-Range Archivist at the Internet Archive (archive.org), offered us an exploration of the challenges, philosophies and implications of archiving digital and social media content. Jason has collaborated on various projects at the Internet Archive, including emulation, imaged software and millions of uploaded items. He co-founded the Archive Team, an activist archiving group.

Fragility and ephemerality

Jason emphasised that much of the internet's content – especially on social media – is inherently ephemeral and therefore vulnerable to loss. He compared the lack of digital preservation standards to a broken social contract, likening it to landlords evicting tenants without notice or recourse. He explained that many social platforms offer no meaningful export or backup options, making user data disposable. This reality makes the need for digital preservation and archiving extra important.

The role of archivists and institutions

Jason and the Archive Team have taken on the role of digital preservationists, often stepping in when platforms shut down with little warning. He explained that this work should ideally be done by governments or institutions, not volunteer groups. Museums and libraries, therefore, have an important role to play in collecting social media and other internet-based content, especially in a volatile environment, where not much is regulated.

Sensitivity

Social media platforms are, he explained, 'hostile' to archiving. They are constantly changing interfaces and resisting data export. Within this context, there exists a tension between public data and personal privacy, and what is technically accessible online for preservation may also be ethically sensitive. Therefore, preservation should be considered alongside the nature of content and the potential future uses that might (or might not) compromise the creator.

Regulation and infrastructure

Jason advocates for a 'boring but necessary' regulatory framework, akin to that used for car-towing services, that ensures users can retrieve their data when platforms shut down. He envisions a future where data-recovery services are standardised and mandated, reducing the chaos of social media shutdowns that occur frequently and without notice.

Museums and curatorial strategy

Museums should focus on representative samples and static captures (screenshots, longplays, recordings), rather than attempting to capture full interactivity. By suggesting this, he stated that institutions should rely on curated datasets, rather than collecting raw data themselves. The result of such collecting will, in the short term, be more meaningful to museums and audiences.

References

Abidin, C. (2021). Mapping internet celebrity on TikTok: Exploring attention economies and visibility labours. *Cultural Science Journal*, *12*(1), 77–103. https://doi.org/10.5334/csci.140

Allaire, C. (2020). This Inuk throat singer is bringing cultural pride to TikTok. *Vogue*. Accessed 23 February 2025 from www.vogue.com/article/shina-novalinga-indigenous-inuk-throat-singer-tiktok

Arrigoni, G. (2021). Born-digital objects and the not so digital challenges for museum collections. Victoria and Albert Museum. Accessed 23 February 2025 from www.vam.ac.uk/blog/projects/born-digital-objects-and-the-not-so-digital-challenges-for-museum-collections

Arrigoni, G. (2022). Big tech heritage: Collecting impossible objects. Victoria and Albert Museum. Accessed 23 February 2025 from www.vam.ac.uk/blog/projects/big-tech-heritage-collecting-impossible-objects

Arrigoni, G., & McKim, J. (2022). Experimentation and collecting practice: Balancing flexible policies and accountability in developing born-digital museum collections. *Museum Management and Curatorship*, *39*(3), 317–334. https://doi.org/10.1080/09647775.2022.2133782

Balsam, J., & Foden, S. (2021). A revival of Indigenous throat singing. *BBC*. Accessed 23 February 2025 from www.bbc.com/travel/article/20210414-a-revival-of-indigenous-throat-singing

Black, J. (2018). Overtone singing: History, development, and influence in contemporary music. Capstone Project thesis, California State University. Accessed 23 February 2025 from https://digitalcommons.csumb.edu/caps_thes_all/402?utm_source=digitalcommons.csumb.edu%2Fcaps_thes_all%2F402&utm_medium=PDF&utm_campaign=PDFCoverPages

Bushey, J. (2016). The archival trustworthiness of digital photographs in social media platforms. PhD thesis, University of British Columbia. Accessed 23 February 2025 from https://open.library.ubc.ca/collections/ubctheses/24/items/1.0300440

Cameron, F. (2021). *The future of digital data, heritage and curation in a more-than-human world*. Routledge.

Craig, S. L., McInroy, L., McCready, L. T., & Alaggia, R. (2015). Media: A catalyst for resilience in lesbian, gay, bisexual, transgender, and queer youth. *Journal of LGBT Youth*, *12*(3), 254–275. https://doi.org/10.1080/19361653.2015.1040193

Crouch, G. (2022). The internet is chaos. It's a reflection of humanity. *Medium*. Accessed 20 April 2024 from https://gilescrouch.medium.com/the-internet-is-chaos-its-a-reflection-of-humanity-9b5477b99ef

Cultural Heritage Agency. (2014). *Assessing museum collections*. Cultural Heritage Agency.

Debono, S. (2021). Collecting pandemic phenomena: Reflections on rapid response collecting and the art museum. *Collections*, *17*(2), 179–185. https://doi.org/10.1177/1550190620980844

Digital Preservation Coalition. (2015). *Digital preservation handbook*. Accessed 23 February 2025 from www.dpconline.org/handbook

Erway, R. (2010). Defining 'born digital'. Accessed 23 February 2025 from www.oclc.org/research/activities/hiddencollections/borndigital.pdf

Ewbank, A. (2017). Democracy sausage: Come to vote, leave with a sausage. *Atlas Obscura*. www.atlasobscura.com/foods/democracy-sausage-australia

Kavanagh, J. (2019). *Contemporary collecting toolkit.* Museum Development North West, Arts Council England. Accessed 27 January 2023 from https://museumdevelopmentnorthwest.files.wordpress.com/2019/07/mdnw_contemporarycollectingtoolkit_july2019.pdf

Knott, J. 2021. *Museum of London acquires viral tweets to document lockdown.* Museum of London. Accessed 30 June 2023 from www.museumsassociation.org/museums-journal/news/2021/02/museum-of-london-acquires-viral-tweets-to-document-lockdown/#

Mata, K. [@Kai Mata]. (2020). I am Indonesian and LGBTQ. X. Accessed 23 February 2025 from https://x.com/kaimatamusic/status/1233037603642859521

Message, K. (2014). *Museums and social activism: Engaged protest.* Routledge.

Nath, I. (2021). An interview with Shina Novalinga. *Air Canada enRoute.* Accessed 23 February 2025 from https://enroute.aircanada.com/en/interviews/shina-novalinga/

New York Historical Society. (2025). History responds. Accessed 23 February 2025 from www.nyhistory.org/history-responds

OCLC. (2024). Demystifying born digital. Accessed 14 February 2024 from www.oclc.org/research/areas/research-collections/borndigital.html

Pearce, S. M. (1994). Objects as meaning; or narrating the past. In S. M. Pearce (Ed.), *Interpreting objects and collections*, (pp. 19–29). Routledge.

Reed, C. (2018). Reviewing significance 3.0. Collections Trust. Accessed 15 June 2025 from https://collectionstrust.org.uk/resource/reviewing-significance-3-0

Renaldi, A. (2024). Indonesia is trying to block LGBTQIA content from the internet. *Rest of World.* Accessed 13 October 2024 from https://restofworld.org/2024/indonesia-broadcasting-law-lgbtqia

Rhys, O. (2011). *Contemporary collecting: Theory and practice.* MuseumsEtc.

Rhys, O., & Baveystock, Z. (2014). *Collecting the contemporary: A handbook for social history museums.* MuseumsEtc.

Russell, R., & Winkworth, K. (2009), *Significance 2.0.* Collections Council of Australia.

Smithsonian Institution Archives. (2025). Digital curation. Accessed 23 February 2025 from https://siarchives.si.edu/what-we-do/digital-curation

Swalwell, M. (2022). The Australian Emulation Network: Accessing born digital cultural collections. Paper presented at *International Symposium on Electronic Art The Second Summit on New Media Art Archiving*, Barcelona, 10–16 June.

Triastuti, E. (2021, 12 March). Indonesian gay communities use social media to break down barriers and stigmas. *The Conversation.* Accessed 23 February 2025 from https://theconversation.com/indonesian-gay-communities-use-social-media-to-break-down-barriers-and-stigmas-156112#:~:text=Indonesian%20gay%20communities%20use%20social%20media%20to%20disclose%20their%20orientation,LGBT%20is%20not%20a%20sickness

van der Werf, T., & van der Werf, B. (2020). Documentary heritage in the digital age: Born digital, being digital, dying digital. In R. Edmondson, L. Jordan, & A. C. Prodan (Eds.), *The UNESCO Memory of the World programme* (pp. 175–189). Springer.

van Dijck, J., & Poell, T. (2013). Understanding social media logic. *Media and Communication, 1*(1), 2–14. https://doi.org/10.17645/mac.v1i1.70

Victoria and Albert Museum. (2022a). *Rapid response collecting.* Accessed 27 January 2023 from www.vam.ac.uk/collections/rapid-response-collecting

Victoria and Albert Museum. (2022b). *Project report: Preserving and sharing born-digital and hybrid objects from and across the National Collection.* Accessed 27 January 2023 from https://vanda-production-assets.s3.amazonaws.com/2022/01/20/12/49/45/92b733d4-929e-429e-9fd1-82d134405465/VA-ResearchReport-Jan22.pdf

Victoria and Albert Museum. (2022c). *Decision model report: Preserving and sharing born-digital and hybrid objects from and across the National Collection.* Accessed 27 January 2023 from https://vanda-production-assets.s3.amazonaws.com/2022/04/26/

16/37/48/f1514821-0884-43dd-ad8c-fd18569b7a7b/VA-ResearchReport-DecisionModels-Mar22.pdf
Victoria and Albert Museum. (2022d). Data modelling for born digital/hybrid objects: *Born Digital, Born Slippery*. Accessed 27 January 2023 from https://vanda-production-assets.s3.amazonaws.com/2022/04/26/16/37/41/ccecc931-4066-4fd8-b17e-63ef22c965f2/VA-ResearchReport-BornDigital-Mar22.pdf
Victorian Collections. (2021). Cataloguing and preserving born-digital items. Victorian Collections. Accessed 23 February 2025 from https://victoriancollectionshelp.zohodesk.com/portal/en/kb/articles/cataloguing-and-preserving-born-digital-items#:~:text=Put%20simply%2C%20born%2Ddigital%20items,only%20in%20the%20digital%20space
Walden, M., & Souisa, H. (2020, 20 February). Indonesia could force LGBT people into rehabilitation under draft 'family resilience' law. *ABC News*. Accessed 13 October 2024 from www.abc.net.au/news/2020-02-20/indonesia-could-force-lgbt-bdsm-communities-into-rehab/11979880
Waters, D., & Garrett, J. (1996). *Preserving digital information: Report of the task force on archiving of digital information*. CLR. Accessed 27 January 2023 from www.clir.org/wp-content/uploads/sites/6/pub63watersgarrett.pdf
Wong, B. (2024). Top social media statistics and trends of 2024. *Forbes Advisor*. Accessed 23 February 2025 from www.forbes.com/advisor/business/social-media-statistics
X Australia [@XAustralia]. (2022). The smell of #DemocracySausage is in the air. X. Accessed 23 February 2025 from https://x.com/XAustralia/status/1513653997902901249?ref_src=twsrc%5Etfw%7Ctwcamp%5Etweetembed%7Ctwterm%5E1513661986856337410%7Ctwgr%5Ec345af493e875433118b0280deb18e031326bfb5%7Ctwcon%5Es3_&ref_url=https%3A%2F%2Fwww.gizmodo.com.au%2F2022%2F04%2Ftwitter-democracy-sausage%2F
Young, R., & McMahon, S. (2021). Shina Novalinga uses social media to preserve, celebrate Inuit throat singing. wbur. Accessed 23 February 2025 from www.wbur.org/hereandnow/2021/04/15/inuk-throat-singing-shina-novalinga
Zuanni, C. (2021). Theorizing born digital objects: Museums and contemporary materialities. *Museum and Society*, *19*(2), 184–198. https://doi.org/10.29311/mas.v19i2.3790

4 Approaches to collecting social media

When a curator or any museum professional is asked about what they do, collecting is at the heart of the conversation. When asked about what and how they collect, there will be a clear narrative that articulates how they go about their work, from researching and identifying significance to the act of collecting, acquiring and accessioning an object. In larger museums, there are dedicated teams of professionals who process objects into collecting institutions. These teams organise transport and movement of objects, receipt the arrival of objects at the physical museum, tag items with specific identification numbers, register them into the collection management system, and responsibly and safely store and control the objects for the term of their life in the collections. In smaller museums, these roles may be undertaken by one or a few people, but the point is that for physical objects, there is generally a clear path in the collection procedures of museums. Born-digital objects, on the other hand, present a range of challenges for museums. As we have discussed, born-digital objects require divergent processes and policies in relation to collection, management, identification, intellectual property and storage structures (Arrigoni, 2021). Social media asks us to rethink collecting practices from curatorial research and significance, which we unpacked in Chapter 3, to the approaches and infrastructures required to collect social media, and then what happens to such objects when they are acquired, ultimately leading to their display and/or a long-term storage solution. This chapter is concerned with collecting approaches – that is, how museums decide to go about collecting social media. At this point, we must acknowledge the reality that there is no one right way to go about it and no agreed-upon best practices. Given the multiplicity of types of social media and the variations across museums (large/small, public/private, specialised/generic), this chapter presents a selection of approaches to collecting social media with the aim of highlighting existing practices, their benefits and their drawbacks. In doing so, we critically analyse approaches to assist museum professionals and others undertaking the task of collecting social media in museums to work out what approach might work best for them and their context.

In this chapter, we present overviews of six areas of collecting: Automated archiving, donated content and data, collecting without collecting, collecting

DOI: 10.4324/9781032669656-4

directly from social media, third-party service provision and simulation. Within each category, we have unpacked examples where social media objects were the focus of collecting activities. Each is analysed by examining the benefits and drawbacks from our perspectives. As stated in Chapter 1, the scholarly field of collecting social media in museums is nascent. While acknowledging work that is likely going on in the museum sector that is yet to be documented, we decided to only use documented examples, and in doing so, our intention is to provide readers and practitioners with insights into each approach that could support collecting social media in a range of contexts. We do not recommend applying any one approach over another; rather, we hope readers will use these examples to better understand the field generally and to work to apply different approaches to different contexts as appropriate to the collecting remit and aims of their museums.

Automated archiving

We use the term 'automated archiving' to describe a technical process designed to automatically capture social media and other web-based content. This often involves using web crawlers or analogous programmes to selectively monitor and harvest large amounts of content identified as relevant for the purpose of collecting and preserving online cultural heritage. It is important to note that automated archiving is not commonly directed at social media but usually targets blogs, websites, government information, journalism and similar content. Over recent years, libraries and archives have started to use whole-of-domain harvesting to selectively collect some social media content, but this is usually limited in terms of its collecting focus (e.g., political campaigns). The Internet Archive and The Wayback Machine, both based in the United States, are two of the most prominent examples of dedicated strategies for collecting and preserving digital content created on and produced for the internet. A related example is from the National Library of Australia (NLA), which houses the Australian Web Archive (formerly PANDORA), comprising collections of websites and publications generally focused on Australian creators and Australian life. The NLA is one of many national libraries around the world responsible for collecting online content deemed to be of national significance, and while its collection development policies vary, more often than not, social media is not explicitly identified. The examples below offer a closer examination of two institutions that have undertaken to collect social media through an automated archiving approach.

Library of Congress, Twitter archive

The Library of Congress in Washington, DC, exemplifies one of the most ambitious approaches to archiving social media. It resulted from an agreement with the influential social networking service Twitter (now X), with the intent of collecting and archiving all public tweets published since the platform's inception in 2006 (Zwaard et al., 2017). The idea of a comprehensive public archive of tweets was a significant acknowledgement of the platform's historical value and status as a place where public debate in general played out online. The Library of Congress does not usually 'collect comprehensively,' yet it made an 'exception for public tweets' for this massive project (Library of Congress, 2017). In its twelfth year of collecting tweets, the library revised its decision and adjusted its strategy to be more selective and target 'events such as elections' and activities or 'themes of ongoing national interest' (Library of Congress, 2017). Despite this change to the scope of its collecting, the library now holds 12 years' worth of tweets, representing one of the most comprehensive collections of social media in the world. However, the collection itself is not currently accessible (Library of Congress, 2017), largely because it poses considerable challenges in terms of the size and complexity of the collection. There are many practical and policy questions yet to be resolved in terms of how to provide access, how to restrict access to certain content and how to deal with issues of privacy (Zimmer, 2015). It is instructive that the library was unable to sustain this collecting approach due to the changing and ephemeral environment of Twitter and the sheer volume of content being produced and collected. The original scope required revision, as at the onset of the project, the library was only collecting text, but given the importance of other content embedded in posts, such as images, links and videos, the purview needed to be expanded (Library of Congress, 2017).

State Library of New South Wales and CSIRO Data 61, social media archive

An Australian example of automated archiving of social media is the partnership between the State Library of New South Wales (SLNSW) and the Commonwealth Scientific and Industrial Research Organisation (CSIRO). This State Library has long collected directly from newspapers, television and radio, but sought to expand to digital sources to gain a greater understanding of public concerns about important topics that manifest online. Working in collaboration with the Data 61 business unit of CSIRO, they developed Vizie, 'a tool designed to collect, analyse and archive social media' (Barwick et al., 2014, p. 5). This interface transferred Twitter data onto a web-based map that contained data visualisations of geographical and emotional information reflecting the people who used the platform in the jurisdiction of New South Wales. The SLNSW identifies keywords and hashtags to collect, then Vizie gathers social media posts that contain these keywords and hashtags from social media platforms, including Facebook, Twitter (X), Reddit and Instagram. Vizie also collects data from social media published in languages other than English, including Chinese, Spanish and Arabic, acknowledging the multicultural makeup of New South Wales. One specific project drawing on this database collection involved working with a not-for-profit organisation dedicated to mental health, the Black Dog Institute. An emotional hierarchy was developed in order to present a full range of emotions communicated via social media on a digital flower. Data on emotions, including joy, sadness, surprise, love, anger and fear, were extracted from users' choice of words in their posts. Interestingly, by using this approach, the library was able to document the community's response to a high-profile siege that took place in 2014 at Sydney's Lindt Café, when an armed man took 18 people hostage, and two people died. Social media posts were later displayed by the library as part of an exhibition alongside other content to demonstrate the impact of the event on the community (Hyland, 2015), highlighting the interpretive capacity of social media content as objects of historical and social significance.

Benefits and drawbacks

For a museum, rather than a library or an archive, the main challenge with automated archiving is that it captures large amounts of content and requires either a limited or broad curatorial approach at the time of collecting. This means that what is collected on archiving platforms results in collections that can be too narrow to be representative versus those that are vastly extensive, making them unwieldy, difficult to sort and challenging to make accessible to museum audiences. Museums, especially social history museums, tend to collect a smaller number of objects with the capacity to communicate multiple stories that can be generalised and extrapolated for interpretive purposes. Therefore, this kind of bulk automated collecting from social media may not suit museum policies and frameworks, as it would involve an unnecessary use of resources to collect and store more than is required to communicate a particular cultural context. However, social media archives such as the Library of Congress and SLNSW might be useful as a research tool to understand a collective response to moments of historical significance and how they play out online.

Another challenge for museums with a specific geographic remit, such as city museums, is that because of the global nature of the internet, collections are necessarily international in scope (Barwick et al., 2014, p. 5). This needs to be considered as part of the cultural context, and museums must make decisions about what to collect in relation to collection policies and frameworks that may need to be reviewed in the context of social media collecting. There are also legislative limitations regarding copyright in different countries. For example, what can be collected with or without user permission will vary across jurisdictions, and, as such, a catch-all approach to social media archiving via platforms that are global is a challenge for collecting as well as for public access and display. This is possibly why the SLNSW presents social media as data visualisation – to protect the privacy of the user. However, for a museum, it may be more compelling to display a post with words and images to capture the online environment and communicate a moment in time, an aesthetic trend and other features of the object in situ. The library and archive sector is doing extremely important work in the space of automated archiving in terms of preserving online culture and heritage, and is technically much further advanced than other collecting institutions. For museums that require greater curatorial oversight when collecting social media, it may be that donated content and data might be the more appropriate pathway for entering the space of social media collecting.

Donated content and data

One way museums are successfully collecting social media objects involves users donating content and data by uploading to digital infrastructures. As a practice, user-donated activities can emerge in response to significant events such as a crisis or disaster or originate from something more trivial, such as everyday observations and representations of a place or behaviour. This approach to collecting social media seeks to capture the lived experiences of extreme events such as bushfires or floods, or more mundane experiences of everyday life, such as observations that emerged during the COVID-19 pandemic. This approach, whereby museums develop web infrastructure, creates and promotes a curatorial call to action, making it possible to have in place suitable parameters for digital-born objects – for example, file size, type, resolution and so on. Importantly, it affords the museum the ability to manage and acquire consent through appropriate processes, thereby overcoming some of the perceived and real obstacles encountered by museums when collecting directly from social media platforms. Potential issues such as who owns the content, how long it will be held for, and what happens if a creator dies can be negotiated at the very beginning of the process.

The digital objects collected using this approach are what we would consider crowd-sourced – that is, rather than being selected by curators intentionally, they are chosen by the user but prompted by a general call to action, theme or topic that a museum communicates. Objects and content collected through a crowd-sourced approach function within a particular context that works to build a group or community account of something the museum seeks to better understand and collect. Usually, these engagements and the objects they yield are displayed online rather than in physical museums or as part of exhibitions and displays. That is not to say that other approaches to display and interpretation are not possible, but rather that museums are still grappling with how to interpret and display digital-born objects in physical spaces.

National Museum of Australia, Momentous: Sharing bushfire and pandemic stories

The National Museum of Australia (NMA) responded to two moments of significant change impacting the country – the 2019–2020 Australian bushfire season and the COVID-19 pandemic – by creating a new web infrastructure to collect stories online (Wilson-Barnao et al., 2023). Prior to this, the NMA had established two separate, yet related, Facebook groups – Fridge Door Fire Stories and Bridging the Distance: Sharing Our COVID-19 Pandemic

Experiences – which attempted to create an online space for Australians to share their personal experiences of major events of disruption. The Facebook groups were extremely popular among users, who seemingly wanted to share their stories and connect with others through likes and comments. This, coupled with the proliferation of social media use during the COVID-19 pandemic, led the NMA to create a dedicated website to collect more stories specific to these events.

Momentous: Sharing Bushfire and Pandemic Stories was launched in October 2021. The project brought together, conceptually, the bushfire season and the pandemic as moments of profound change and invited users to share their personal experiences related to either or both. In contrast to third-party social media platforms, *Momentous* asked users for considered responses and detailed reflections, selections of images, audio and video content. Users gave titles to their posts, 50-word descriptions to their images and multimedia content, and allocated qualities to their stories – for example, hope, sadness and worry. *Momentous* enabled online users to read, view and reflect on shared experiences, irrespective of their participation through the submission process. In this way, participation was defined by users actively submitting stories, alongside engaging with content passively. Over 300 stories were collected that spoke to deeply personal, yet collective experiences of Australians through extreme challenges and profound change. Upon posting their submission to the site, users were required, through checking boxes, to give their permission to the NMA to technically acquire their content and reuse and republish their content in a range of ways and on a number of different platforms. What this project underscores is the desire for people to share their stories digitally and via social channels. However, the NMA's project also signalled a desire for some people to donate their stories for long-term preservation. This was never the original intention of the *Momentous* project, as the content is not part of the museum's National Historical Collection. Rather, it will become an official record of the agency's creative output, given that it was conceived as a digital engagement activity. Nevertheless, it successfully shows museums a pathway for collecting social media through the development of web infrastructures that are owned and controlled by the museum.

Museum on Main Street: Stories from Main Street

As part of the Smithsonian Institution's travelling exhibition function, Museum on Main Street (MoMS) seeks to connect mostly Washington, DC-based museums and collecting institutions with 'small-town America' through a range of products and programmes. One way of doing this is through the *Stories from Main Street* project, which encourages Americans to share life stories in response to an invitation by the MoMS with the following provocation:

> We're interested in your stories about life in small-town America. Our goal is to create an archive of stories that show the excitement, diversity,

> and complexity of American life. We want to feature the best stories offered by people all over the country in future Museum on Main Street exhibitions and on this website. We know that your experiences make the stories that the Smithsonian tells even richer. Work with us to elevate knowledge of rural America!
>
> (Smithsonian Institution, 2016a)

The MoMS began collecting stories via the internet in 2011, gathering audio, photos, text and videos from everyday people living in small towns in the United States. Thousands of Americans have contributed their stories to the programme, leading to the display and resharing of stories on social media platforms, in podcasts and in travelling exhibitions. The focus of collecting is thematic and changes regularly. Recent research focused on water, sports teams, rural homes and democracy. While not specifically articulated by the MoMS as social media collecting, many of the stories include digital cultural artefacts that could be considered social media, including born-digital social photography and videos. Much like *Momentous*, this approach to collecting stories digitally allows for control of digital collections by museums, including permissions to reuse and republish. The MoMS articulates in the submission guidelines that users 'will retain ownership of your submission, by submitting content you give the Smithsonian (and those authorized by the Smithsonian) permission to use it for educational, promotional, or other non-commercial purposes' (Smithsonian Institution, 2016b).

National Library of New Zealand: Facebook archive programme

In 2019, the National Library of New Zealand (NLNZ) invited New Zealanders to donate their Facebook archives to their website as part of its 100th anniversary celebrations for the Alexander Turnbull Library. The NLNZ acknowledges that its 'personal digital files are inherently interesting to future generations but are also transitory and subject to the whims of corporations' (Love, 2020). The institution describes the collecting project as designed to assist future researchers in viewing 'what we chose to save, how we used social media platforms like Facebook, and to better understand the rich context of early 21st century digital life and culture' (National Library of New Zealand, 2025). The overall aim was to collect data from 100 accounts to develop a collection that represented a broad cross-section of the community and represented its relationship to Aotearoa New Zealand and the Pacific. The NLNZ accepted donations via its website, where users were asked to download their Facebook archive, fill out a donation form and submit using the online interface. Donors were able to restrict the level of access, choosing either to make it unavailable to researchers for 25 or 100 years or to restrict its access only to researchers onsite in the secure reading room. This approach gave agency to the donor and reduced perceived barriers to donating personal data.

Benefits and drawbacks

The NLNZ used donated data to collect and archive social media, avoiding some of the issues that the Library of Congress encountered in an automated archiving approach by limiting the scope of the collection, along with access to it. The records the library collected document everyday engagement with social media in an uncurated form. In contrast, projects such as *Momentous* and *Stories from Main Street* adopt a donated data approach but elevate the role of collecting institutions in shaping the acquired social media. The NMA and MoMS created new spaces, outside of third-party social media platforms, to collect social media and/or digital stories. These institutions offered online audiences a call to action and asked users to curate and interpret their content. In some cases, users may have created content specifically for the respective websites, rather than digging through their social media archives or resharing what they had already posted on other social media platforms. With *Stories from Main Street*, the museum submission page clearly signalled that they only sought stories of relevance to the current themes, and any contributions outside of this would not be included. This begs the question of authenticity and the ways in which museums can ensure the authenticity of content. It is unclear whether a call to participate will impact an authentic social media object and its place in a wider historical narrative, despite the perceived benefit to the museum regarding permission, content and even the technical aspects of collecting the content. It also raises questions about whether user content donated to museum-owned infrastructure alters its status as a social media object. These are issues with which the museum sector needs to continue to grapple as it embarks on such collecting activities, and this necessarily involves interrogating the nature of objects. We contend that there are no right or wrong answers in this complex and changing space, and we encourage museums and those collecting social media to document not only social media objects as things in their own right but also the context in which they existed at a point in time and the ways in which they were collected so such objects can be understood and read in contextually specific ways in the future. All these examples required museums to either have or create digital infrastructure. We know this might not be possible for some museums, but that does not mean social media cannot be collected.

Collecting without collecting

Another way to collect social media is not to collect it at all. What we mean by this is collecting social media without collecting born-digital objects or artefacts. The purpose of this type of collecting is to record a particular phenomenon, moment in time or event that involves human interaction with social media. Museums can do this by inviting users to share stories, testimonies, oral histories and so on related to their use and engagement with social media. The intention of this kind of collecting, in general, is not to display what is collected so much as to use the power of social media as a storytelling device that can help to shape the understanding and context of a particular period of human experience, where the internet and social media are shaping and being shaped by expressions of culture. This approach can be especially useful when a museum is attempting to document and communicate stories of solidarity. It is where individuals connecting on social media become transformative citizens because their connectedness and visibility can lead to change in the form of a social or political movement. In this context, social media storytelling becomes empowering for users as it creates new possibilities for groups to mobilise and reshape inequities and injustices. From the museum's perspective, this can afford opportunities to incorporate the voices of individuals and communities as it seeks to understand multiple perspectives on a particular social, cultural or political issue, which in turn plays a key role in shaping the curatorial narrative. This approach can include provision for contributors to remain anonymous and to have their content archived for research purposes rather than exhibited as objects. This strategy imports logics from oral history, a methodology of historical inquiry that involves 'extended, recorded interviews undertaken for a particular purpose and often with a view to eventual archiving for preservation and public access' (Oral History Australia, 2023), but can be instructive for museums and collecting institutions.

Nordiska Museet, #MeToo collection

The Nordic Museum (Nordiska Museet) in Stockholm began collecting digital stories in 2015 through its website minnen.se. The website contains personal stories, photos, drawings, films and audio recordings submitted by online audiences. The museum has since released around 20 questionnaires across a variety of different subject areas, garnering approximately 10,000 submissions. With an intention to document experiences from the #MeToo hashtag campaign, the museum prompted online audiences with the following questions:

> Have you posted anything, or shared, on social media in connection with the #MeToo campaign? Have you participated in any manifestation on the theme, for example where you live? … Tell us about your experience of it, and how you participated or contributed. [Translation from Swedish to English]
>
> (Nordiska Museet, 2025)

The museum's website-based collection approach allowed individuals to remain completely anonymous, attach their location or include their year of birth – all of which were voluntary pieces of information. Participants had the choice to display their responses publicly or archive them for researchers. The collected materials are not strictly social media objects, as we have previously articulated, but rather a collection of stories, oral histories or testimonies. These stories augmented the museum's existing collection around sexual abuse, and at the same time allowed the museum to collect oral histories and testimonies that say something important about human interaction with and use of social media in the context of social justice and contemporary activism campaigns. While this project did not collect social media as a digital cultural artefact, it presents a useful way for museums to consider collecting human experiences of social media to ensure that the human relationship is documented for future generations. In addition to understanding collecting social media without collecting social media as oral history, we can see its alignment with physical collecting. In a moment of shifting ideas about the status of born-digital artefacts, there are examples – much like in the collecting of film and cinema stories – of museums focusing on the physical evidence related to digital heritage. This approach should be considered alongside collecting social media objects conceptually and technically, or as a first step for museums to better understand how social media interfaces with their focus or current collecting policies.

Benefits and drawbacks

The Nordic Museum's #MeToo project relied on existing audiences who already contributed to the online life of the museum to submit oral history and testimony about their engagement with a social media phenomenon. The project clearly possesses social and historical value, but it is instructive in the manner that it applies logics of physical and analogue collecting to born-digital contexts. The museum is able to articulate human experience with digital tools and technologies, including social media, but does not attempt to understand or collect social media as digital cultural heritage. This example, however, raises questions around reliance on existing museum audiences and consideration of whose voices might not be heard in employing such an approach. While there are no simple answers, this is an important caveat in adopting novel approaches to collecting to question who is being included and who is being excluded as a result. Museums should carefully document their decision-making processes so that historical records are clear and context-rich to ensure that social media objects – or, in this case, individual narratives about social media – can meaningfully be appraised. Avoiding misunderstanding of context in the future will ultimately shape how people understand moments and cultural phenomena of the past.

Collecting directly from social media

A more direct method of approaching social media collecting is the museum actively seeking out, identifying and collecting content directly from social media platforms and, if necessary, negotiating permissions for use and republication directly with the creator. There are many ways in which this can take place, and we have identified two primary ways that an institution might approach this type of collecting. The first is for the curator to search platforms for content that relates to a person, event or theme that they seek to document and collect. This relies on the curator using existing search engine infrastructure and functionality, established by the third-party social media platforms, which vary significantly across social media platforms. The challenge with this approach is that the curator can be left searching for a needle in a haystack, using hashtags or key terms in a saturated repository of information and content. It can be difficult to narrow down what is important from such a large corpus of content. When working in this way, it is best to use a museum-owned device for searches to limit algorithmic intervention – for example, using personal devices and accounts will skew the content being delivered, based on past interactions online with the search engine and its algorithmic memory. Of course, there is potential for bias in all collecting, as curators have lived experiences that inform how they view and understand the world; these can impact collecting physical artefacts and decisions about what is significant or not. Regardless of the ways in which curators search for and identify content on third-party social media platforms, there is great benefit to collecting directly from social media because of the way it communicates creator intention, use, reaction and response, visual and brand aesthetics, the user environment and so on. These are the elements that are missing from previously discussed approaches, which would enrich the social media object and provide multiple ways for museums to engage with and interpret such content online and in gallery contexts. The following examples, while technically more challenging, demonstrate the value of investing in infrastructure and resources and collecting directly from social media platforms.

Science Museum Group: An absolute unit

On 9 April 2018, the Museum of English Rural Life (MERL) in Reading, United Kingdom, posted on its Twitter account an image of a hefty-looking ram accompanied by the words 'look at this absolute unit' (Museum of English Rural Life, 2018). The post went viral. The museum explained that 'on day one, our Twitter followers had increased by more than 50% … and the tweet itself had surpassed 68,000 likes and 20,000 retweets' (Koszary, 2018). That post is still live on the platform X (formerly Twitter) and has received more than 95,200 likes. The image has been reused and remixed as an internet meme hundreds of times. This phenomenon of the internet meme is what another museum has collected. The Science Museum Group (UK) worked with researcher Arran Rees to collect the meme as 'one of the most significant and famous examples of meme culture in the UK' (Science Museum Group, 2018). Rees (2021) explains that a meme is not one object but something that is continually reimagined as it morphs into a cultural practice as well as an object type. Given that the Science Museum Group is dedicated to science, deciding on what to collect and why was important. Rees (2021) observes that memes and memetic culture are linked to the development of photography, which has been radically changed in the social media environment, so it was important to capture how photography is presented in this context. It was also decided that a series of four posts would best represent how memetic culture plays out online – that is, how the 'absolute unit' post was reshared and remixed with the inclusion of comments and text with every reposting. Rees (2021) explains that the Science Museum Group drew on digital preservation approaches such as 'significant properties' – identifying the characteristics of the digital object/s that, to be understood and accessed over time, must be preserved – to work through how to collect the meme. The object, as it is catalogued by the Science Museum Group, is a WARC or Web ARChive file format, which combines multiple digital resources into an aggregate archive file together with related information. The object was captured using Connifer web recorder software to show the meme in the context of the Twitter interface. Rees, as the curator, moves through a planned series of clicks that is recorded to demonstrate how the meme was posted and responded to on the X platform.

Australian Centre for the Moving Image (ACMI): Succession

To engage audiences in a discussion about the acclaimed television series *Succession* and its fanbase, the ACMI web-recorded a YouTube post by Liminalist titled '*Succession* but it's a Romantic Comedy (Trailer) Tom and Greg' (ACMI, 2024). The YouTube video draws on footage from the television series to generate a comedic trailer for a romantic movie starring Tom Wambsgans and Greg Hirsh. ACMI uses the video to engage audiences in a discussion about the show's fanbase and about how the video became viral thanks to a group of fans, 'TomGreg shippers,' who speculated that the relationship between the two characters on the satirical comedy drama was more than platonic. The institution did not seek the creator's permission to display the video, but does credit its creator. This decision was based on an understanding that the object is not the 'original' but a recording of an interaction with the object. Therefore, a risk-management approach was taken that credits the appropriate author, yet does not seek permission because what is being presented is not the original object. The video can be viewed onsite at ACMI as a result of the institution's relationship with the Australian Emulation Network. However, due to rights and access requirements, it can only be viewed as a screenshot on the museum's website. While the recording is not in ACMI's official collection, it is used as an interpretive aid to demonstrate an approach to using social media for interpretation and display.

Museum of London: #CitizenCurator

The Museum of London (MoL) has perhaps been the most experimental institution when it comes to collecting social media. One project run in conjunction with the University of Westminster demonstrates a direct collecting approach. Through the project #CitizenCurator, MoL sought to capture a more complete account of the 2012 Olympics as the event was taking place and to obtain a broad cross-section of the experiences of London residents. To do this, MoL established a hashtag, #CitizenCurator, so it could track the content being produced from the much larger corpus of Olympics tweets. The initiative ran as a physical exhibition, an online blog and a Twitter handle (Ride, 2013). To circumvent potential intellectual property issues associated with collecting from another social platform, the museum selected Twitter (now X) and did not collect user-generated photography (Ride, 2013). The museum sought to broaden its collecting remit by issuing a call to the general public to participate via Twitter, the museum blog and various websites (Ride, 2013). MoL successfully recruited volunteers, who agreed to ensure that there was enough content on Twitter to engage audiences by posting daily. To encourage broad representation of these volunteers, they were recruited from different parts of London and held varying attitudes towards the Olympics. Every day, a cross-section of tweets posted to social media was then selected by citizen curators and posted to a Storify page. Collecting around 8500 unique tweets (Aravani, 2021), the initiative effectively captured a representative account of the event and documented important conversations taking place at the time (Miles, 2013). The museum displayed the #CitizenCurator collection onsite through a temporary exhibit alongside other objects collected during the 2012 Olympics, as well as a film that included some of the tweets, providing a deep social history of the city during this period (Miles, 2013). What is significant about this approach to collecting social media is that while a hashtag was employed as a strategy to track content, there was clear curatorial oversight because of the agreed-upon process and the inclusive call to action.

Benefits and drawbacks

ACMI's presentation of a YouTube engagement demonstrates that, in a digital era, objects are multifaceted and can be reappropriated, where a scene from a television show can be rewritten and embedded with new meaning, then shared by users on social media. ACMI displayed a significantly altered object that played with the identity of the key characters. In this way, social media allowed the museum to collect multiple perspectives in one object (a screen/web recording) and document the views of different people associated with it through the capturing of user interactions. The screen recording made it possible to share stories of individual people (the fanbase) and how their association with a particular television series manifested online in a playful way. The object is less about the television series and more about human interaction and use of social media, and how networks – human and otherwise – come together because of it. For museums, this reveals how the social media object is not always self-evident or what the museum might initially seek to collect (a user post), depending on the intention of collecting. This idea pushes museums to really consider the logics of social media and the internet as they relate to collecting intentions. As Arran Rees (2021) reminds us, memes are a great example of how museums must adjust to this type of collecting, as social objects are embedded with multiple meanings and challenge traditional understandings of authorship and ownership. This approach to collecting raises significant challenges, both in terms of a general approach to collecting social media content and with regard to display without user permissions and/or the awareness of users as to the intention of keeping social media screen recordings as objects in perpetuity as part of a museum collection. In addition, as researchers globally experienced with the rebranding of Twitter as X, platform-based environments are constantly changing, making this approach challenging in the context of authenticity – for example, the look, feel and functionality at the time of posting and/or specific interactions.

By contrast, #CitizenCurator took a user-first approach to direct collecting activity. That is, the user was aware of their social media interaction and the intentions of the museum to collect and interpret content, and ultimately gave permission to MoL to use and republish content in a variety of formats. For long-term preservation, a user-first approach is important, but the drawback is that when users are led by a curatorial call-to-action, it may impact their posts. This raises questions about the authenticity of the content or whether users self-censored in this instance – or indeed whether it matters in the context of generalising an experience of Londoners on social media responding to a major sporting event in their city. This begs the question of what exactly authenticity means in an online context that straddles private lives and digital public space, and the performative culture cultivated by such a space. These are all matters with which museums need to grapple when collecting social media and understanding such digital cultural objects within their contexts, and not in comparison with other cultural contexts. The three examples presented here evidence the value of collecting directly from social media platforms but confirm the need for increased resourcing and the creation of new digital infrastructures.

Third-party service provision

An alternative way to collect born-digital and social media objects that has emerged in recent times is through platforms created by third-party service providers. This approach draws on a collecting infrastructure that is not owned by a museum. Instead, it is initiated by a third party and invites users to upload their donated content. This kind of relationship between a museum and a third-party provider can be considered in the same way as many collection management systems are – that is, the infrastructure is not created by museums but used by them and serviced through a contractual agreement. Such providers can offer simple and fast solutions to museums that may not necessarily have the time or resources to create or maintain their own web infrastructures, enabling them to undertake social media collecting.

Connect to Collect

One paid service that takes responsibility for meeting the General Data Protection Regulation (GDPR) rules, an initiative of the European Union designed to protect individual privacy and limit personal data use (Burgess, 2020), is Connect to Collect. In 2014, a new aspect of the GDPR was introduced, known as 'The Right to be Forgotten,' which means that an individual can request their personal content be deleted from the internet. However, according to the current legislation, an organisation 'archiving in the public interest,' such as a library or archive, is not obligated to remove this content if it is decided to be of 'enduring value' (National Archives UK, 2024). If the content is of significant public value, there is no onus on the collecting institution to keep those records 'up to date in the same way as data still subject to operational use' (National Archives UK, 2024). However, this doesn't mean that collecting institutions are not responsible for instigating practices that protect individual privacy, and it is clear that when collecting social media, they need to be wary of financial or physical loss or the possibility of 'substantial distress' (National Archives UK, 2024). Balancing the right to information versus the right to privacy is a complex and serious issue for collecting institutions in a digital age. Connect to Collect (2025) provides museums moving into social media collecting with greater confidence through a third-party approach that makes it possible for audiences to directly load their content to a system, which can then be viewed in a gallery or online. The benefit to a museum is that the hosting and storage of social media content is preemptively managed by the provider, reducing the institution's overall risk in terms of data management. The Connect to Collect (2025) system assists with the integration of social media content into the institution's archive system. Individuals who upload their social media content create an account and can then decide on the content they would like to make visible and have the option to later revise any decisions about what they have displayed by unpublishing a particular image or collection. Notably, only participants in a particular group can view content if required, and translations can be added for multilingual audiences (Connect to Collect, 2025).

Benefits and drawbacks

Third-party providers such as the Connect to Collect platform offer a simple and accessible way for museums to collect social media. This approach reduces the potential financial and resource-intensive risk associated with born-digital collecting to museums that many museums may not be able to easily accommodate. Much like museum-owned web platforms, the collected born-digital objects may or may not have been published on social media platforms. Indeed, services working to collect social photography may be collecting photos created specifically in response to the service and/or from people's smartphones – photos that, until they are uploaded, may have never been seen in a social context. This requires museums to be diligent in their understanding of the content and the object and to ensure that the interpretation of such objects does not mislead viewers about the object's status as a social media object. In such cases, the method of collecting must be comprehensively documented to allow for appropriate interpretation and understanding of the object over time.

Simulation

Approaches that involve simulating a social media environment differ greatly from what has been discussed so far. Rather than directly replicating a media platform, this method works to 'simulate' aspects of its 'operations and thereby provides insights into the patterns that emerge from and feedback into this process' (Burgess et al., 2022, p. 9). The overall aim is to make user participation on social media more apparent, or to highlight aspects of a media platform's design, where machine-based systems shape their everyday experiences and practices. This approach is focused on understanding the phenomenon of social media rather than a user communicating something. It acknowledges that what is being received by social media users is an important part of the cultural practice. In this way, simulation helps to overcome the practical and ethical limitations involved in social media collecting because it aims to simulate an environment by pulling together content and data (in some cases, for a limited amount of time) to reveal information about technical and cultural processes. It also flips the conversation to acknowledge that our current culture and history are being shaped by the intersection of people and computational technology.

Victoria and Albert (V&A): WeChat collection

The Victoria and Albert Museum sought to collect WeChat with an aim to preserve and highlight its unique functionality and design, which allows users to access multiple apps in one place. In 2015, the museum approached WeChat to explore the possibility of its inclusion in the permanent collection (Cormier, 2017). The museum identified two key obstacles to the collecting initiative. First, collecting the APK file (a file format used by the Android operating system) would be a major issue, as it would be difficult to hold the object due to the risk that the server could become obsolete in the future (Cormier, 2017). Second, the content loaded to the social media platform contained personal information that, from a preservation perspective, presented substantial legal and privacy challenges. In consultation with WeChat, a decision was made to collect a replica of an offline demonstration model of the social media platform, drawing on a version that initially was created for the Apple App Store. The benefit of this version of the app was that it did not require a server to function. To overcome the need to incorporate real user content, WeChat created a fictional character, Star (Cormier, 2017). To make Star appear authentic and to replicate the user experience, WeChat loaded photos, contacts and other relevant content such as chats. At the time, the museum also collected drawings and 'GIF files of their Bubble Pup sticker series' as the character was 'an unofficial mascot' for the social platform, which was the first to introduce the use of GIFs in this context (Cormier, 2017). Despite the fact that the phone that houses the simulated app has full functionality, the museum chose not to display the phone in its gallery in Shenzhen but instead to exhibit a video of someone using the app demonstrating its functionality, given that visitors 'have the same functionality on their phones' (Cormier, 2017).

The Australian Advertising Observatory

The Australian Advertising Observatory is an example of critical simulation that relies upon users donating social media data (Burgess et al., 2022). While not directly targeted at collecting for a memory institution, this initiative of the Australian Research Council (ARC) Centre of Excellence for Automated Decision-making and Society uses citizen scientists who use a plugin that collects sponsored advertising content, which they then donate to the project. Given the individualised and fleeting nature of advertising on Facebook, the Australian Advertising Observatory is an important example of donated data because it makes temporarily available a collection of advertisements, which in turn makes this content available for researchers to analyse. This project is significant, as it has collected over '750,000 advertisements from more than 2,000 users,' and, as a result, has successfully identified Facebook advertising for the gambling industry that breaches Australia's *Interactive Gambling Act 2001*, which prevents casinos that operate outside the country from advertising (Parker et al., 2023, p. 3). To achieve this outcome, the researchers searched for terms about gambling, such as 'casino,' 'slots' and 'pokie,' and sought to determine if the gambling services were not prohibited under the Act by identifying the location of the advertiser and double-checking it against a 'list of blocked gambling websites maintained by the Australian Communication and Media Authority (ACMA)' (Parker et al., 2023, p. 3). While this collection is temporary, it does successfully present an alternate approach whereby it becomes possible to make visible the hidden decision-making behind an AI-based model that enables personalised advertising to hold social media platforms more accountable.

Benefits and drawbacks

The most apparent drawback of simulation is the technical and financial impact on museums of undertaking the work. The benefit of simulation, however, is that it allows museums to overcome some of the legal and ethical issues they encounter when collecting social media. Both the V&A museum and the data observatory used simulation to explore the design and behind-the-scenes practices. Simulation presents a radical approach to acquiring social media that acknowledges that authenticity in the digital space is not as clear-cut as it is with physical objects. Copies, replicas and simulations have a role in communicating social media in a cultural context. There is an argument to be made that many born-digital artefacts are indeed copies, yet unlike in the art world, copies are not inauthentic. When it comes to social media, museums can collect objects at a moment in time that will continue to circulate online for years to come. A seminal example is the 'absolute unit' social media post collected by the Science Museum Group, which still has a life online. If museums can shift their thinking beyond the limits and logics we apply to physical collections, the idea of collecting social media becomes a possibility. Simulation helps us to understand this and to shift the value proposition of museum collections and objects from rare, one-of-a-kind treasures to something more.

Conclusion

In this chapter, we have articulated six approaches to collecting social media in museums – automated archiving, donated content and data, collecting without collecting, collecting directly from social media, third-party service provision and simulation – while considering the benefits and drawbacks of such approaches. We have put forward 12 separate examples drawn from contemporary museum practices that highlight key ways for museums to proceed in the future in collecting social media content. Each example has provided an insight into the challenges and opportunities of collecting social media. While the challenges are many, we believe the benefits outweigh the drawbacks. No matter which approach is taken, it is clear that it is possible to collect social media right now – and we encourage it!

To conclude, we want to articulate the role of the curator as important to the creation as well as the collection of social media objects. Since the beginnings of museums as institutions, curators have played a significant role in deciding what does and does not make it onto the official record of history, as well as being the caretakers of material culture over time. Of course, the practice of curators historically has been critically analysed, yet the role persists to exist with ever-changing and more expansive perspectives on the practice of curators from sole expert to cultural mediator and collaborator, and this role becomes even more important in the realm of the internet and social media. Social media is inherently relational – to interact with social media means to bring yourself, as a curator, to bear on what you are engaging with. Social media platforms use generative AI to determine what you may or may not be interested in, and these algorithms determine what is seen and what is not. This means that the supposed neutrality of a curator is called into question. In the world of social media, we must accept this bias and document it. We must also acknowledge the role of the curator in creating social media objects that are informed by algorithmic bias and where certain comments, ads, likes and shares will be displayed above others. Furthermore, when using technologies such as web recorders, the curator has a central role in determining what is recorded, often being the person who clicks through content as it is being recorded. Regardless of which approach is taken to collect social media, including those articulated in this chapter, the role of the curator is present. From deciding where and for what content to deploy web crawlers, to developing and distributing a call to action to online users, to literally clicking through content while screen recording, the curator is an active participant in the creation of social media objects, and this is something the sector needs to acknowledge and that needs to be comprehensively documented to understand such heritage into the future.

Insights from practitioners

Keir Winesmith and Bronwyn Dowdall

> We cannot take [a collect] everything approach. So, we need to take an intentional approach.

Keir Winesmith is the chief digital officer at the National Film and Sound Archive (NFSA). He holds a PhD in new media and a science degree in computer science and physics, and is the co-author of *The Digital Future of Museums* (2020) and the co-founder of the Sydney Cultural Data Salon.

Bronwyn Dowdall is the senior manager of NFSA enterprises and was formerly the chair of Copyright in Cultural Institutions (CICI). Bronwyn leads the enterprises team at NFSA, which includes access, rights and licensing. Her work focuses on navigating the complex legal and ethical terrain of copyright, donor relationships and digital rights management.

Four approaches to collecting

Keir and Bronwyn shared with us how the NFSA is thinking about collecting social media. From their perspective, there are four approaches to collecting. The first, they explained, is like spearfishing – this is where you see one item that you think is important and you grab it, and that is it. It is collected, divorced from its social media context, documented, interpreted and stored. The second approach is more like fishing: You throw a line out there and hope to catch something. You plan on objects coming to you, rather than seeking out specific objects – you might collect a few things when fishing, add them to a collection, document them and make sure the rights and permissions are sorted. The third approach, they explain, is like a dam: You collect all the fish that can fit in the dam, and maybe that dam is everything created from a geographic location, everything created on a platform in a specific year or everything on a certain topic. You try to catch it all – which they assert is perhaps not the right solution for medium- to small-sized institutions, and sometimes not for large ones either, as it requires significant resourcing. The fourth approach, and the one in which the NFSA is more interested, is compared to a bucket. Buckets are not comprehensive and rather include objects that are content-rich and can communicate specific stories that are also representative of culture, community and history. Buckets do not just include the social media post but also the reactions to the post, the experience of interacting with that post on the social media platform, a documented understanding of why the creator made the post and any physical collections that might relate to it.

The bucket approach, according to Keir and Bronwyn, is not only achievable for cultural institutions but also develops collections that are more meaningful to audiences.

Policies are important

In 2024, the NFSA made a purposeful decision to pause AI projects as an organisation so it could co-develop a value framework with staff designed to emphasise trust, public value and transparency before resuming work. The NFSA is approaching social media collecting in the same way. The aim is to make a principled stance on what, why and how the NFSA collects social media, one that builds on its existing collecting policy.

Donor relationships are critical

The NFSA's reliance on donations to build the collection makes trust paramount to any kind of collection use, they explained. This is the case for many museums, and it is important to recognise that missteps in rights management can damage relationships and potentially impact future collecting efforts. It is therefore important to assess copyright implications upfront. While not all rights issues will be resolved, assessment can support stakeholder management.

Nic Carah

> Data donation is a kind of flipping of the ethos … it's better than scraping, because it's based on an agreement with people … a much more ethical and durable way of going about collecting this ephemeral digital culture.

Nicholas Carah is a professor at the University of Queensland and the director of the Centre for Digital Cultures and Societies. He is a member of the Australian Internet Observatory (AIO), a national research infrastructure designed to enhance Australia's capacity to collect, analyse and understand the data housed on social media platforms.

Distinguishing between observatories and archives

In our interview with Nic, he distinguished between building observatories and creating archives. Observatories, in his view, are dynamic, real-time systems designed to understand the flow and context of digital culture, while archives imply static, long-term storage. He expressed that archives raise ethical, ecological and interpretive challenges in the context of social media – which, as he explained, was often intended to be intimate and ephemeral when it was originally created and shared.

Challenges of archiving algorithmic and ephemeral culture

Nic highlighted the difficulty of preserving digital culture shaped by algorithms, such as memes, TikTok trends and dynamically generated ads. These forms resist traditional archival methods because they are constantly changing and context-dependent, raising questions about what and how to collect for future understanding. He advocated for platform observability and tools and processes that allow researchers and the public to understand how platforms shape culture. Ethical social media collection can include data donation rather than just scraping media platforms, according to Nic.

References

ACMI. (2024). What if *Succession* was a rom com? Accessed 23 February 2025 from www.acmi.net.au/works/122312--what-if-succession-was-a-romantic-comedy

Aravani, F. (2021). The new museum's personality: Digital collecting as a way to democratize museums. *Medium*. Accessed 26 February 2024 from https://medium.com/@hlossi/the-new-museums-personality-digital-collecting-as-a-way-to-democratize-museums-37efc4aa3dd3

Arrigoni, G. (2021). Born-digital objects and the not so digital challenges for museum collections. Victoria and Albert Museum. Accessed 29 December 2024 from www.vam.ac.uk/blog/projects/born-digital-objects-and-the-not-so-digital-challenges-for-museum-collections?doing_wp_cron=1735426101.2406229972839355468750#:~:text=In%20fact%2C%20the%20challenges%20of,ownership%2C%20crediting%20and%20managing%20expectations

Barwick, K., Joseph, M., Paris, C., & Wan, S. (2014). Hunters and collectors: Seeking social media content for cultural heritage collections. Paper presented to *VALA2014 17th Biennial Conference*, Melbourne.

Burgess J., Andrejevic, M., Angus, D., & Obeid, A. (2022). *Background paper: Australian Ad Observatory*. ARC Centre of Excellence for Automated Decision-Making and Society. https://doi.org/10.25916/7BGE-BP35

Burgess, M. (2020). What is GDPR? The summary guide to GDPR compliance in the UK. *Wired*. Accessed 13 March 2024 from www.wired.co.uk/article/what-is-gdpr-uk-eu-legislation-compliance-summary-fines-2018#:~:text=The%20full%20GDPR%20rights%20for,automated%20decision%20making%20and%20profiling

Connect to Collect. (2025). About Connect to Collect. Accessed 23 February 2025 from https://connecttocollect.org/about

Cormier, B. (2017). How we collected WeChat. Victoria and Albert Museum. Accessed 15 May 2014 from www.vam.ac.uk/blog/international-initiatives/how-we-collected-wechat

Hyland, A. (2015, 11 December). NSW State Library used social media to record Martin Place siege. *Australian Financial Review*. Accessed 23 February 2025 from www.afr.com/work-and-careers/management/nsw-state-library-used-social-media-to-record-martin-place-siege-20151210-glk7o1

Koszary, A. (2018). *How an 'absolute unit' of a tweet catapulted one rural life museum into the spotlight*. University of Reading. Accessed 23 March 2024 from https://research.reading.ac.uk/research-blog/2433-2

Library of Congress. (2017). Update on the twitter archive at the library of congress. Accessed 5 March 2024 from https://blogs.loc.gov/loc/files/2017/12/2017dec_twitter_white-paper.pdf

Love, V. (2020). Saving your social media. National Library of New Zealand. Accessed 23 March 2024 from https://natlib.govt.nz/blog/posts/saving-your-social-media

Miles, E. (2013). Tweets in the opening Olympics in #Citizen Curators Life in London during the Games. Citizen Curators. Accessed 27 February 2023 from https://citizencurators.wordpress.com/

Museum of English Rural Life [@theMERL]. (2018). Look at this absolute unit. X. Accessed 23 February 2025 from https://x.com/TheMERL/status/983341970318938112?lang=en

National Archives UK. (2024). Archives and GDPR: Frequently asked questions. Accessed 16 March 2024 from www.nationalarchives.gov.uk/archives-sector/legislation/archives-data-protection-law-uk/gdpr-faqs/#:~:text=What%20is%20the%20'right%20to,purposes%20in%20the%20public%20interest

National Library of New Zealand. (2025). Facebook Archive Project. Accessed 23 February 2025 from https://natlib.govt.nz/collections/donations/donating-digital-items/facebook-archive-project

Nordiska Museet. (2025). Me Too. minnen. Accessed 23 February 2025 from https://minnen.se/tema/metoo

Oral History Australia. (2023). What is oral history? Accessed 25 February 2024 from https://oralhistoryaustralia.org.au/guidance/what-is-oral-history

Parker, C., Albarrán-Torres, C., Briggs, C., Burgess, J., Carah, N., Andrejevic, M., Angus, D., & Obeid, A. (2023). Addressing the accountability gap: Gambling advertising and social media platform responsibilities. *Addiction Research & Theory*, *32*(4), 312–318. https://doi.org/10.1080/16066359.2023.2269852

Rees, A. (2021). Remixing museology: An approach to collecting social media in museums. PhD thesis, University of Leeds. Accessed 23 February 2025 from www.google.com/search?q=aaron+rees+thesis&rlz=1C1GCEA_enAU1101AU1101&oq=aaron+rees+thesis&gs_lcrp=EgZjaHJvbWUyCQgAEEUYORigATIHCAEQIRiPAtIBCDI0MjhqMGo3qAIAsAIA&sourceid=chrome&ie=UTF-8#:~:text=An%20approach%20to%20collecting%20social%20media%20in%20museums

Ride, P. (2013). Creating #Citizencurators: Putting Twitter into museum showcases. In K. Cleland, L. Fisher, & R. Harley (Eds.), *Proceedings of the 19th International Symposium of Electronic Art*, ISEA2013, Sydney, Australia. Accessed 23 February 2025 from http://ses.library.usyd.edu.au/handle/2123/9475

Science Museum Group. (2018). Absolute unit Twitter meme. Accessed 23 March 2024 from https://collection.sciencemuseumgroup.org.uk/objects/co8796558/absolute-unit-twitter-meme-an-internet-meme-composed-of-a-black-and-white-photograph-of-a-large-ram-absolute-unit-twitter-meme

Smithsonian Institution. (2016a). Share your story – *Museum on Main Street*. Accessed 23 February 2025 from https://museumonmainstreet.org/stories/share/register

Smithsonian Institution. (2016b). Terms and conditions for submissions – *Museum on Main Street*. Accessed 23 February 2025 from https://museumonmainstreet.org/content/terms-and-conditions

Wilson-Barnao, C., Middleton, C., & Enright, L. (2023). Redefining crisis in museums: Insiders' perspectives on digital engagement. *Curator: The Museum Journal*, *66*(2), 351–365. https://doi.org/10.1111/cura.12546

Winesmith, K., & Anderson, S. (2020). *The digital future of museums: Conversations and provocations* (1st ed.). Routledge. https://doi.org/10.4324/9780429491573

Zimmer, M. (2015). The Twitter Archive at the Library of Congress: Challenges for information practice and information policy. *First Monday*, *20*(7). https://doi.org/10.5210/fm.v20i7.5619

Zwaard, K., Aydelott, M., Brunton, D., Crawford, M., Grotke, A., Marcou, N., Mears, J., Nagel, J., Potter, A., Rago, M., Short, S., & Sweeney, J. M. (2017). Institution as social media collector: Lessons learned from the Library of Congress. IFLA WLIC 2018 Kuala Lumpur, Malaysia. Accessed 5 March 2024 from https://library.ifla.org/id/eprint/2428/1/093-zwaard-en.pdf

5 Ethics and collecting social media

One afternoon, as I (Caroline) waited to collect my son from school, I dialled 321 (Australia's voicemail service number) on my smartphone to listen to a voicemail. My father had died five months earlier, and I had asked him to leave me a message that I might hold onto so I could hear his voice. Until this day, I had resisted listening to it – perhaps in part pretending that he hadn't died. Dialling 321, I was surprised to hear that I had no saved messages. This couldn't be right? I had just listened to my messages at lunchtime, and I had six voicemail messages. How could the messages have disappeared so suddenly and without me doing anything? I called the phone carrier and was greeted by a nice young man in a call centre, presumably on the other side of the world. He was moved by my predicament and told me that he, too, had saved multiple voice messages from his grandmother, who was terminally ill, so that he might listen to her after she died. I sat with bated breath as he spoke with his supervisor, but despite both their best efforts, there was nothing that they could do to save my messages, which it seems are housed on the device itself. The man in the call centre suggested that I look at the deleted messages section of the device, but failing that, suggested I seek out a phone expert locally who might know how to retrieve it. Stunned and disappointed, I returned home and discussed the situation with my 16-year-old daughter, who promptly started searching the internet for answers. We were surprised to find that I was not alone and that millions of other people encountered the same problem as a result of an iOS 17.4 update. In a discussion thread on an Apple forum, user after user expressed their deep sadness at losing cherished messages from family and friends that were automatically deleted. I had assumed that my voicemail was safe and that I could maintain the message on my phone as long as I liked until I was ready to hear it. Like me, the other users in the forum used the voicemail on their phones as a place to keep cherished memories, a space to access a technology that made it possible to retrieve important moments central to their own experiences and histories. Smartphones allow us to communicate despite where we are and whatever we are doing. Until that moment, I hadn't experienced firsthand what losing a mediated memory feels like. I would never hear my father's last words of advice and wisdom because I had

DOI: 10.4324/9781032669656-5

wrongfully assumed they were safely preserved somewhere between the hardware of my phone, the cloud and the carrier.

We are reminded by Australian Centre of the Moving Image (ACMI) CEO Seb Chan, in his International Council of Museums (ICOM) address, of the fragility of digital objects as they 'exist in systems that require reliable power, engineering, maintenance, [and] ongoing software development' (Chan, 2022). The experience of digital data loss in the online space is common in the twenty-first century. These losses range from file-saving errors or corruption, lost or forgotten passwords, power outages, bank and platform shutdowns or more sinister disruptions such as viruses or terrorism. These kinds of losses impact individuals, businesses, governments, nations and museums. This reality, as Elizabeth Merritt (2025) explains, is critically important to museums, whose missions often centre on preservation. While perhaps one of the most concerning realities of collecting in the digital realm, this is one of a few key areas that require consideration by museums when collecting social media.

This chapter explores some of the more complex ethical challenges of collecting social media in museums, including storage and sustainability, privacy and protection, commercialisation and corporate players and synthetic media. First, we consider what and for how long user content is stored by media platforms, and what implications this has for collecting and environmental sustainability. Second, we explore the rights of users in the context of privacy, including the Right to be Forgotten and how that might impact collecting activities. Third, we highlight the role of commercialisation and corporate players in the social media ecosystem and how they can influence the decisions museums make when deciding to collect social media. Fourth, we consider the implications of synthetic media, including how artificial intelligence is changing the social media landscape and how that might influence museums' collecting strategies in the future. These ethical challenges are not easily resolved, and they call for new ideas, approaches and policies to better support museums in collecting social media with confidence. It is no longer possible for museums to rely solely on their existing practices and frameworks to undertake the work of collecting social media responsibly and ethically. Alongside unpacking these ethical challenges by drawing on existing scholarship, we have also turned to today's major social media platforms and reviewed their policy documents, pointing to some of the ways in which they impact museums that are attempting to collect social media. By doing this, we aim to highlight what museums must consider when collecting social media.

What follows asserts the need for museums to build ethically informed practices and principles for collecting social media that acknowledge the complexity of the online space, are respectful of the individuals and communities that museums intend to document and serve, and that are grounded in contemporary values. These practices and principles may be contextually specific to each museum or collecting institution, yet they always exist in relation to the context of social media cultures. What is discussed here will support museums to better understand the wide-ranging considerations that impact their core business in general. This chapter should not be understood as a guidebook that will assist museums in addressing or solving each and every ethical issue related to collecting social media. Indeed, there are scholars, technologists, policymakers and others whose work is centred on such endeavours. Ultimately, as institutions that seek to document human experience, museums must not ignore the complex challenges of social media but rather consider how to collect within a complex environment that is in a constant state of change. Rather than attempting to get it right from the outset – dot all the I's and cross all the T's – we assert that if museums consider the contexts and ethics and apply good principles to their practices, responsible collecting will follow.

Storage and sustainability

Storage – the housing of collections, either physically or digitally – is one of the most pressing issues faced by museums in the twenty-first century (International Council of Museums, 2024, p. 49). The challenges associated with storage are not only about space but also cost – financial and environmental. Digital storage, while it sounds simpler to achieve than physical storage, requires a huge amount of physical and digital space and massive hardware and software costs. Furthermore, any digital services museums maintain contribute to an institution's carbon footprint – this includes powering servers, laptops, monitors, Wi-Fi and more (National Archives, 2023). As museums increasingly turn digital – from collections to exhibitions and experiences – their data storage needs will grow, and so will their environmental impact. Collecting social media will contribute to data storage and to a museum's carbon footprint. Perhaps more concerning in the context of this book is the way social media is currently stored – on platforms – and what that means for museums that want to represent social media cultures in their collections.

Social media content is stored on third-party media platforms. These platforms act as gatekeepers of important digital cultural heritage. This role is not necessarily one that was intended when media platforms were created. However, given the increasing acknowledgement that digital output is cultural heritage, the role is one that now serves to prohibit collecting institutions such as museums from collecting and documenting social media. There is a tendency by creators who create and share content on social media to think that what they publish on social media platforms is safely stored in a similar way as we might once have considered family photos safe by being glued into albums and placed into cupboards. This is not the case, and it is somewhat naive of creators to assume that they will always have access to their social media content and archive. This is, of course, a general statement, and many creators back up and store their content – but many people still do not, and this is a significant problem. At the end of the day, social media platforms are not accountable for the long-term storage and preservation of content produced on or through their platforms. Nor are they subject to the same level of regulation as legacy media, including print, radio and television.

While it is true that social media platforms are not required to retain all data, it is also difficult to know what data they do hold onto and for how long. For museums, this makes it especially difficult to ascertain how long social media content is being kept before it is deleted and ultimately lost to the historical record. The social media giant Meta, for example, in its retention policy states:

> We keep information for as long as we need it to provide our products, comply with legal obligations or to protect our or others' interests. We decide how long we need to keep information on a case-by-case basis.
>
> (Meta, 2024)

How might museums interpret 'for as long as we need,' and what might this mean for the pace at which museums might need to collect content housed on Meta platforms? Another major platform, WeChat, states in its Terms of Service that:

> We do not permanently retain chat data on our servers and it only passes through our servers so that it can be distributed to your intended recipients. Chat data is only stored on your device and the devices of the users that you have sent communications to.
>
> (WeChat, 2025)

This suggests that access to chat histories on WeChat – potentially important correspondence – is vulnerable to the fate of the creators' devices. These statements provide an inconsistent approach to data storage: One does not indicate how long they will store what they hold, and the other suggests that they do not hold data on their servers at all. It is, however, highly likely that social media platforms do not want responsibility for long-term data storage of what they house, given the expense and significant infrastructure required to do so. This context makes collecting and preserving social media particularly challenging for museums. Specifically, if museums do not have a clear understanding of how long social media content is kept by platforms, they are unable to strategically plan to collect content that may be significant in the future but requires time and distance to fully understand its ongoing significance, as is the case for many objects that are collected through contemporary collecting initiatives. What this suggests is that, without clarity from platforms collecting social media, a rapid-response approach is required in order to mitigate the risk of loss. Not all museums will be able or willing to take on such an approach; however, museums must ask themselves what they are sacrificing if they decide not to collect.

Another consideration is how storage by platforms influences the ways museums collect social media. If museums are unaware of how content is stored, and specifically in what form, they might not be able to determine which approach to take or which technology to use when undertaking to collect social media content. For example, is content archived by media platforms at the time of posting? Is it archived in a way that captures the online environment? Do data and content archived by platforms evolve over time with updates to the media platform's branding and functionality? Or are the data archived by social media platforms disconnected from their public interface and stored as fragments of data (text, links, code)? These are all questions that museums will need to ask when determining how to collect and when. These considerations also intersect with questions of significance – that is, which aspects of the social media object require authenticity by means of replication (e.g., the web environment it was posted to at the time of publication), and which are considered suitable for change (e.g., the device or player on which a social media object can be viewed in the future). Within this storage context, the collecting of social media is far from straightforward, and museums must be prepared to consider more complex ways of keeping, caring for and displaying social media objects – ways that might not apply to physical objects and in some cases contradict the ways in which museum professionals and conservators are taught to care for material culture.

Museums must also keep in mind that social media has a footprint that extends beyond the internet, which incorporates assemblages of devices, servers and physical products (Casemajor, 2015). Behind every piece of content posted to social media is a vast digital infrastructure that includes servers – which are notoriously damaging to the environment due to the significant amount of electricity they require to function (Crawford, 2021, p. 43). This is largely due to the cooling systems used to maintain them, which greatly increase greenhouse gas emissions. In a global context, where many organisations are changing their practices to meet obligations to reduce carbon emissions and become environmentally sustainable, museums must be cognisant of the environmental impacts posed by collecting and storing born-digital objects, including social media. In response, while it may be easy to suggest that collecting social media is unethical within this context, we do not believe that museums can ignore the significant cultural output of social media, so they must collect it, but must do so with environmental impacts in mind. In this way, moving away from an archive-it-all approach, which we have already identified as unsustainable, is an ethical approach. Museums, in our view, should be selective and intentional about what social media they collect and why – that is, they should collect social media as representative of context, moments, trends and more. Social history museums are already good at this. They select objects that at once can tell a personal, sometimes localised story, and at the same time can tell a more generalisable story of human experience, intended to connect with a broad audience. This approach to collecting in museums becomes more important through an ethical lens of storage and environmental sustainability and relies on those building social media collections to make strategic decisions about what social media to collect.

Privacy and protection

Most museums – especially those attached to governments – have strict policies about how to manage the use of personal information of those who donate physical objects to the institution. In the same way that the privacy of donors of physical artefacts is protected, so too should the privacy of online creators who post their content to social media and whose content the museum intends to collect be protected. It is therefore important for museums to understand the context in which social media content is published online. While creators give consent for media platforms to use and reuse what they publish, they do not necessarily anticipate that their content will be held in perpetuity with the potential for their content to be reused, shared or sold online. They are also not considering the possibility of museums collecting or copying their content for long-term preservation and use. Because most social media platforms include provisions in their terms of service to hold creator content in perpetuity but are unlikely to do so, there is also a false sense of permanency of digital information, especially from the perspective of the creator. Museums must be aware of this and be critical of the terms and conditions of different platforms, which are seeking the best possible outcomes for their business, but should not be interpreted by museums as regulations and/or protocols that are strictly adhered to. A critical lens over terms and conditions and the evolving contexts of social media platforms will ultimately benefit museums as they navigate collecting.

Conceptually, social media is ephemeral, and the underlying premise of it is that creators keep posting to share thoughts and feelings, to communicate news, to entertain themselves and others and to convey lived experiences in real time. When social media creators communicate using media platforms, they are not necessarily thinking about the long-term ramifications of handing over control of their content and data. This is mostly because few people make time to review a platform's policies before they sign up, and they can misunderstand the amount of control the platforms have over their content. For example, some creators upload photos of their children's development to social media, understanding their use of a platform as a digital diary, with the assumption that their photos will be kept safe by the platform forever (or for as long as the creator wants) and that the publishing and reuse of such photos are controlled by them. However, in reality, such content can be subject to reuse under different circumstances. Some social media creators are indeed concerned about the reuse and repurposing of their content by third parties, whereas others do not appear to mind, or they simply do not know. This can be impacted by an individual creator's digital literacy. For example, younger social media creators are becoming increasingly more adept at adjusting privacy settings, while older users are less concerned about the visibility of their content online and focus more on building connections (Edwards, 2019). Referring to Facebook's privacy settings, Dominique Glassman (2020, p. 48) points out that 'users know that their content is public to people in their network, but they are less aware that their personal disclosures are being collected and processed by Facebook and its platform partners, often for financial gain.' While most media platforms ascertain that users own the content that they post to social media, by sharing it in this space, they ultimately lose control of how it is used, repurposed and reshared. For example, Instagram's Terms of Use state:

> When you share, post or upload content that is covered by intellectual property rights (such as photos or videos) on or in connection with our Service, you hereby grant to us a non-exclusive, royalty-free, transferable, sublicensable, worldwide licence to host, use, distribute, modify, run, copy, publicly perform or display, translate and create derivative works of your content (consistent with your privacy and application settings). This licence will end when your content is deleted from our systems. You can delete content individually or all at once by deleting your account.
>
> (Instagram, 2024a)

At first glance, it looks like the licence for the platform to use the content ends when a user deletes their personal content or deactivates their account – but this is not the case. Instagram's privacy policy also makes it clear that when a user deletes content from their account, this process takes some time to complete. Similar to other platforms, Instagram (2024b) states that

> copies of your content may remain after the 90 days in backup storage that we use to recover in the event of a disaster, software error or other data loss event. We may also keep your information for things such as legal issues, terms violations or harm prevention efforts.

This means that even after a creator has deleted content, it is impossible for the creator to know whether their content remains in the platform's systems. So, while Instagram does not own an individual's intellectual property, it holds a licence that allows it to use creator content in accordance with its own terms of service, and that has the potential to impact a museum's capacity to collect, use, republish and exhibit social media content in a range of contexts.

To better understand how these terms of service, policies and licensing agreements might cause challenges for museums and other collecting institutions, especially as it relates to the control platforms have on what is essentially a historical record, we turn to a recent example. Meta's social media platform, Instagram, was being used to conduct citizen journalism in response to the violence taking place as a result of the Israel–Hamas war, which we mentioned in Chapter 1 as an example of historically significant material being produced and shared on social media. Palestinian citizens and well-known activists used their Instagram presences to document the impacts of the war as it was unfolding daily and in their own communities. This included the posting of graphic images and footage of bombings, the shooting of Palestinian people, and the physical impacts of the war on everyday people, including children. What resulted was mass takedowns of content that had been published to the social media platform by Palestinians and their supporters across the globe due to Meta's graphic content rules and regulations (Human Rights Watch, 2023). This kind of interference is not new or exclusive to online environments – for example, there are many cases of diaries of artists and well-known people that have been donated to museums with pages ripped out of them, often by families to conceal some of the more salacious details of a personal life. Similarly, the control that corporations such as Meta have when it comes to access to content, and the ability to enact a range of interference such as takedowns and censorship, have ramifications for museums in understanding, documenting and collecting a wider context of social media. From a loss perspective, it also means that, after content is taken down, creators – the owners of the intellectual property – can potentially no longer access it in its social media environment. While many people still produce content outside of platforms and post it later, many use the functions of applications to take photos or videos, edit and post, so there is a risk of complete loss. Ultimately, the social media platform maintains control of what content is made available and for how long. This kind of intervention by the platform makes it challenging for museums to not only collect specific content but to know how much of what they/we are seeing on platforms has been influenced by a platform's management decisions. Another major platform of the twenty-first century, TikTok, articulates in its Terms of Service that the company assumes no responsibility for maintaining the content housed on the platform:

> We shall not be liable to you for … The deletion of, corruption of, or failure to store, any content and other communications data maintained or transmitted by or through your use of the services … without our express written consent, for any commercial or unauthorized purpose.
>
> (TikTok, 2024)

So, alongside decisions being made by platforms about what is and is not available to consume online, and for how long, many platforms also take no responsibility for deletion, corruption or failure to store content produced by their users. Policies such as those articulated here raise ethical concerns for the platforms themselves but also bring attention to the precarious contexts in which social media content and objects exist.

Another privacy consideration is the Right to be Forgotten, a right under the European Union and the United Kingdom's General Data Protection (GPD) law, 2014. It is significant, as it establishes a new avenue through which individuals can request that their data be removed from websites, including search engines and social media. Even though some data need to be held by media platforms to meet legal obligations or to protect the public interest, this law provides greater control for users over the content they share online. It enhances protections around individual privacy in a digital age, which has implications for European museums, where there is now a greater onus to obtain creator consent and procedures to seek erasure of data. Museums should ensure that the data they hold do not cause damage or distress to individuals, and they need to develop robust data-management policies that inform creators about how their information will be managed in the future. This entails obtaining informed consent and permission from people who are recognisable in photos and videos and saving a record of their consent. As Jason Scott, archivist and software curator at Internet Archive, highlights, years later, individuals might look back on their social media content from a different point of view:

> I am no longer this gender. I am no longer this name. I don't wanna have this brought up in school. I don't wanna have this brought up on my job that I used to run the really awesome furry art page. I wanna remove that, you know, because, of course, companies are more and more using vendors that are doing cross connections.
>
> (Scott, 2024)

Within the context of the Right to be Forgotten, a range of contexts exist in which a data subject can request their data to be deleted (General Data Protection Regulation, 2025):

- the personal data are no longer necessary for the purpose an organisation originally collected or processed them
- an organisation is relying on an individual's consent as the lawful basis for processing the data, and that individual withdraws their consent
- an organisation is relying on legitimate interests as its justification for processing an individual's data; the individual objects to this processing, and there is no overriding legitimate interest for the organisation to continue with the processing
- an organisation is processing personal data for direct marketing purposes, and the individual objects to this processing
- an organisation processed an individual's personal data unlawfully
- an organisation must erase personal data in order to comply with a legal ruling or obligation
- an organisation has processed a child's personal data to offer their information society services

An organisation also has rights, so the Right to be Forgotten can be overridden (General Data Protection Regulation 2025) if:

- the data are being used to exercise the right of freedom of expression and information
- the data are being used to comply with a legal ruling or obligation
- the data are being used to perform a task that is being carried out in the public interest or when exercising an organisation's official authority

- the data being processed are necessary for public health purposes and serve the public interest
- the data being processed are necessary to perform preventative or occupational medicine. This only applies when the data are being processed by a health professional who is subject to a legal obligation of professional secrecy
- the data represent important information that serves the public interest, scientific research, historical research or statistical purposes, and erasure of the data would be likely to impair or halt progress towards the achievement that was the goal of the processing
- the data are being used for the establishment of a legal defence or in the exercise of other legal claims

While the Right to be Forgotten does not extend beyond Europe at the time of writing this book, we inhabit an environment where there is increasing recognition of the need for an informed strategy about how to process and maintain social media collections. What this means, or might mean, for museums is a refocusing on deaccessioning policies and programs specific to born-digital material produced by creators on the internet, including social media. Deaccessioning is not new, and it happens all the time. Decisions about what is removed from a museum's collection are varied – from the detection of hazardous materials to repatriated material culture to duplications, especially in relation to type examples (French & Smith, 2024). Deaccession decisions are, of course, subject to robust processes to ensure that any decision to remove an object from a collection is carefully considered, scrutinised and documented. However, most deaccession processes are internal. So, when it comes to the Right to be Forgotten, a piece of legislation that supports creator agency online and acknowledges the complexities of the internet, what implications will this (and other future policies and regulations) have for museum collecting practices? Are museums prepared to radically shift their power dynamics, especially as they relate to collection management, to ensure that internet and social media content, and its future in museum collections, are embedded with creator agency? And if so, what does that mean for deaccessioning processes and decisions? This is where consent, permissions and licences become increasingly important for museums. Risk of deaccessession can be mitigated through clear consent processes, which are lacking in some approaches to collecting social media that we have discussed previously. Nevertheless, museums and all collecting institutions will need to grapple with how the logics and social norms of the internet and social media subcultures will be applied to collecting practices. This applies not only to deaccessioning but also to how, at the outset of collecting, social media creators fully understand what their content entering a museum collection means in the long term.

While we endorse the need for increased literacy associated with privacy online, we also note that increased privacy, security and the Right to be Forgotten make social media more challenging to document by museums. This context means less content is available for public consumption, so museums are exposed to much less social media content that may be historically or culturally significant. There are parallels for museums collecting physical objects or having access to the private lives of donors, where items of cultural significance are held in private domains, and their existence is sometimes unknown to professionals working in museums. When museums move to collect social media, it is therefore imperative that they develop an understanding of the context of the ecosystem – specifically, the ways in which platforms and individual creators are influencing access to content. This is important when it comes to the interests of researchers, historians, curators and future generations wanting to better understand the phenomenon of social media and its relationship to human experience. This context should then be documented. The decisions made by platforms – for example, censorship and/or takedowns – and which creators make – requesting content removal as per the Right to be Forgotten – will inform a cultural context in which collections are acquired and subsequently continue to exist and be understood. These impacts need to be documented by museums at the time of acquisition to ensure that when platforms and contexts no longer exist, collections in museums can be interpreted in contextually specific ways that fully communicate how the content came about and what factors influenced its life online. This is about ensuring social media objects can be understood fully by future generations and not misunderstood or treated as the singular, unchanging fact or truth of an entire group of people.

Commercialisation and corporate players

Social media platforms and the creators who populate feeds are increasingly commercialised. Celebrities, high-profile individuals and thought leaders monetise their content and influence on social media, and increasingly more ordinary people – creators – are participating in influencer marketing cultures and even becoming non-traditional celebrities (Zhang, Liu & Bi, 2022, p. 1). This results in sales and marketing, paid partnerships, subscription services and more. Social media is also a viable form of employment for many people, and this is increasingly becoming the case. What does this mean for museums? First and foremost, museums participate in this social media subculture – they market exhibitions and events, sell tickets online and facilitate cross-promotion and paid partnerships. They also work with influencers to spread their content and message. None of this is bad, but the commercial context of social media requires further scrutiny by museums when they seek to collect authentic creator content. As the non-traditional celebrity rises through the ranks, to what extent are their personal reflections representative of social media culture broadly and of those whose profiles are much smaller or private? We are not suggesting that influencers are inauthentic and not worthy of collecting – indeed, museums should collect influencer content. However, content collected in a highly commercialised context should be interrogated and documented to ensure that context is not lost. Furthermore, museums should not lose sight of the seemingly unremarkable content created by those who are not trying to sell or gain commercially, to ensure that complexity exists within a historical record of social media. Whose content is collected and whose is not is an ethical consideration for museums when working to reflect human history and culture as played out on social media.

More than those creating and publishing content, it is also easy to forget the reality that social media collecting practices operate in a context dominated by powerful corporate entities. These players do not just own the platforms, but they also control the granular-level features that platforms deploy, including emojis, filters and music. While users may believe that everything applied to content on a social media platform is open for our use and will not be changed after it is posted, this is not necessarily the case. At the beginning of 2024, Universal Music Group had a feud with the social media platform TikTok when an agreement between the two companies ended on 31 January the same year. Penning an open letter to the social media platform, Universal Music explained that 'in our contract renewal discussions, we have been pressing them on three critical issues – appropriate compensation for our artists and songwriters, protecting human artists from the harmful effects of AI, and online safety for TikTok's users' (Universal Music, 2024). By the end of January, Universal Music had removed its artists' music and restricted access to high-profile performers such as Billie Eilish and Harry Styles to put pressure on TikTok to pay more to use its content and to reduce the use of artificial intelligence (AI) to generate music (Rogers, 2024). For around three months, content circulating on the social platform that used Universal Music suddenly became quiet, and the meaning deeply embedded in the content circulating on the platform became lost until a new agreement was reached in May. The high-profile argument highlights the extreme vulnerability of content housed on social media platforms and the opaqueness of behind-the-scenes corporate decision-making (Strauss, 2024). As we have already explained, social media content is complex and can comprise many parts – including text, photos, videos, audio, filters and more – and when one of those parts is compromised, the meaning of the content can be altered and past iterations of the content obscured from new consumers. The muted posts from the short-term pulling of some of Universal Music's popular artists represent the alarming extent to which social media content can be destroyed and damaged. While one could argue that the muted posts say something about corporate politics and are something to be collected, the contrary impacts should also be noted. Other kinds of social media content suffer from such moves, including posts associated with conflicts and trauma. Alongside the potential copyright challenges associated with parts of a social media object being owned by multiple corporate players, the need to acquire quickly becomes even more apparent. Museums must be cognisant of this and potentially create methods of acquisition that allow for rapid-response collecting to occur. This, of course, raises challenges associated with significance, which changes over time, and copyright, which can take lengthy periods to acquire. Museums may need to rely more on flexible acquisition and deaccessioning practices when it comes to collecting social media to ensure collections are relevant in the long term and possible to acquire in the short term.

Synthetic media

Not all content is created by humans, so to understand what museums might collect, we need to be more aware of the technological context in which the production of content on social media platforms is now taking place and to understand the implications for determining what is authentic creator-generated content and what is not. We use the term 'synthetic media' (van der Sloot & Wagensveld, 2022) to capture the use of AI tools such as ChatGPT and Dall-E to create realistic images, videos and stories and highlight the increasing adoption of these technologies by museums around the world, which has been a fundamental shift in how museums engage audiences. The use of digital technologies by museums is not new (Kenderdine & Sanderhoff, 2020, Kenderdine & Yip, 2019; Kidd, 2014), and it remains important to acknowledge the evolving challenges they present (Murphy & Villaespesa, 2020). For example, for its *Dali Lives* exhibition, the Dali Museum in St Petersburg, Florida, collaborated with advertising agency Goodby, Silverstein & Partners to create a deepfake of the long-dead artist. Drawing upon archival footage to generate his facial likeness, along with the voice of an actor who read out content from archival interviews and letters (Lee, 2019), the museum created a unique encounter for its visitors. Upon entering a booth in the museum, visitors could listen to Dali recount different stories and even take a selfie with him to share on their social media (Lee, 2019). While this example of the use of deepfake technology is an engagement outcome rather than a collecting initiative, it demonstrates how the networked nature of the internet has facilitated new types of museum encounters, creating new forms of meaning associated with such encounters and what might one day be something worthy of collecting by a museum.

Technologies, like those used to create the deepfake Salvador Dali, are making it easier than ever to create and alter content online. Because of this, there is a greater need to ensure the authenticity of the content that a museum collects. The proliferation of misinformation and fake news on social media also needs to be factored into an institution's overall approach to collecting. There is now a range of sites where users can create fake social media posts, and social media accounts are regularly cloned by cybercriminals. To determine authenticity, museums must investigate an object's documented history, track its provenance and inspect or test its materiality. This process is not without precedent and is applied to all objects donated, purchased or otherwise gifted to a museum. Yet, despite the best efforts of collecting institutions, forgeries of artworks still exist, as do fake antiquities. While the idea of establishing authenticity and provenance has long been a concern, the digital age brings with it new challenges, so it is likely that museums will continue to encounter such issues when collecting social media and internet-based content and require new methods of authenticating objects.

Given this, it is not surprising that the development of synthetic media has created new ethical challenges for museums (Jobin et al., 2019; Landsberg, 2004; Mihailova, 2021). Consider, for example, the increased distribution of manipulated images, videos and audio content on social media aimed at influencing voters in elections. Deepfakes are used to mimic public figures and movies to generate convincing content and play an outsized role in the spread of disinformation (Bode, 2021, 2022). As advances in deepfake technology continue to accelerate, museums will need to mitigate against the potential misuse of this technology (for fraud, propaganda, disinformation or disrupting democratic processes) and consider new criteria that determine what qualities or characteristics should be present in a social media object for it to be considered collectable in the first place (Vaccari & Chadwick, 2020). This is not to say that synthetic media is not something of interest to museums. For instance, a museum seeking to engage audiences in a discussion about the use of this technology (and its potential to cause significant harm) might go about acquiring a deepfake. However, people who have been the subject of a deepfake video may feel exploited, ashamed and embarrassed by its creation. While the person referenced in the deepfake does not necessarily appear in the video, there is an ethical obligation to seek their permission before displaying the fake item publicly, rather than assuming that because it is in the public domain and created by synthetic media, it can be collected and displayed without consent.

A high-profile example emerged in 2024 when the Princess of Wales experimented with editing a family photo supplied to the media and the public by Kensington Palace on Mother's Day. Her editing endeavours were responded to vociferously on social media, claiming conspiracy theories or couching them in satire, and many memes appeared. This media storm raises important matters of trust and norms. While simple edits (via filters and other manipulations) to a family photo are something that smartphone technology enables all of us to do, there are no clear social norms around the practice. When it involved the royal family, the conversation shifted from editing and graphic design to the status of the institution. Joshua Habgood-Coote, a Research Fellow in Philosophy at the University of Leeds, explains that 'producing and disseminating accurate and properly contextualised images is fundamentally about ensuring well-placed trust in competent sources' (Habgood-Coote, 2024). These ethical considerations are apt for museums, as they are institutions that rely on being trusted sources of accurate information. This is not to suggest that museums should not collect such content – in fact, collecting a series of responses to the controversy over the royal image could illuminate a cultural phenomenon associated with social media, and so is worth collecting. Museums, though, must accept responsibility for public education about the reasons for collecting such content and ensure that robust documentation is gathered to explain the context. Cultural institutions ought to be involved in the collection and display of synthetic media, deep fakes and other content generated by AI. However, this practice needs to engage with issues of consent and claims of authenticity, which signal a whole new range of challenges with which museums will ultimately have to grapple.

Applications of AI and machine learning are not limited to deepfakes in social media but also include captions, images and follower responses generated by technologies such as ChatGPT or Midjourney, for example. In response to these developments, TikTok released a tool to assist creators with labelling Edited Media and AI-Generated Content (AIGC) content and introduced community guidelines around the use of AIGC, stating, 'We require you to label AIGC or edited media that shows realistic-appearing scenes or people. This can be done using the AIGC label, or by adding a clear caption, watermark, or sticker of your own' (TikTok, 2025). In 2023, the company also said it was testing out a new label that would apply to all AI content that it automatically detected and that it had partnered in the creation of an industry-based best practice code called 'AI's Responsible Practices for Synthetic Media' (TikTok, 2023). Facebook, Instagram and Threads have similarly acknowledged the need to identify AI-generated content more consistently, and Nick Clegg, President of Global Affairs at Meta, has indicated that it will endeavour to label AI-generated content appropriately. Clegg highlights the continued blurring of 'human and synthetic content' and says Meta has been 'applying "Imagined with AI" labels to photorealistic images created using our Meta AI feature' and that this would be used for 'content created with other companies' tools' (Clegg, 2024). As no common standards currently exist for identifying AI-generated content, Meta has developed a system for identifying photorealistic images using 'visible markers' on the image itself, as well as 'invisible watermarks and metadata embedded within file images' (Clegg, 2024). While the initiatives of some social media companies in recognising the need to identify synthetic media and doing something about it are laudable, museums cannot necessarily rely on such companies to continue to do this work, especially as the rise of synthetic media grows. This raises a suite of challenges associated with authentication when attempting to represent content by humans in museums. Museums must think more deeply about how such technologies will change their existing practices and what new capacities and literacies are required to undertake such work.

While there certainly are instances of AI use that almost everyone will agree provoke ethical concerns around authorship and originality, legislation surrounding its use in most countries has not caught up yet with the pace of the industry itself. This has not prevented cultural institutions from using AI technology (admittedly mostly in a public engagement context), sometimes to their detriment. For example, in April 2024, the State Library of Queensland in Brisbane, Australia, launched an AI veteran chatbot, 'Charlie,' in conjunction with technology company Talkvia to commemorate ANZAC Day in an attempt to educate the general public about war (Gillespie & Nicolas, 2024). The chatbot drew on multiple sources from the library collection and Trove to generate responses and was imagined as a 19-year-old soldier from rural

Queensland. Yet, within 24 hours of its launch, internet users were gaming the bot and testing it out by asking it to impersonate the science fiction character Dr Who and television personality Fraser Crane (Gillespie & Nicolas, 2024). The library's desire to enhance user engagement with its collection by giving the chatbot a personality blurred the line between human and machine – a line that was playfully challenged by the library audiences, highlighting the reality that humans are interacting with technologies more than ever before. The enlarged role of chatbots in navigating public life cannot be overlooked, especially in the context of Meta's recent commitment to introducing AI chatbots to all its apps and devices. Using a similar logic of anthropomorphism, the company explains on its website that it has partnered with a series of high-profile influencers that range from Paris Hilton to Snoop Dogg, 'because interacting with them should feel like you are talking to familiar people' (Meta, 2023). Increased availability of AI-generation tools has made it easier to create avatars that, in many ways, are preferable to influencers and creators, as they can be programmed to endorse whatever message a brand wants, giving advertisers more control. These synthetic influencers cannot merely be dismissed as not being human, as they have started to amass millions of followers, with social media marketing company Sprout Social reporting that '46 percent of Gen Z would be more interested in a brand that worked with an influencer generated by AI' (deLuna, 2024). There also exist fake followers, or bots, that supply sham engagement in the form of likes and comments. The phenomenon of fake influencers and followers makes it especially difficult to generalise how a museum might approach collecting social media, likes, follows, virality and hard statistics do not necessarily mean what they once did, especially as they relate to social, cultural and political impact on social media platforms. What they do help us to consider, though, is how these non-human interactions shape our experiences, relationships and styles of expression online. Museum curators need to consider the non-human actors as much as human ones as part of social media ecosystems that lead to human/non-human interactions and engagements that may be worthy of collecting. This scenario begs for a critical lens to be placed on the content produced, the interactions with the content, and the reception of that content on and offline to ensure that decisions about what is collected by museums are meaningfully understood, documented and communicated to museum audiences.

Despite difficulties in governing the practices of social media platforms, the European Parliament adopted the AI Act in a world-first attempt to regulate its use in March 2024 (European Parliament, 2024). The Network of Museum Organizations (NEMO), writing on the implications of the legislation for its constituency, highlighted three areas of development to enable museums to develop the necessary 'expertise and knowledge' to engage with AI moving forward (NEMO, 2024). Most importantly, there was a call for a 'political vision for museums and cultural heritage in an AI-driven society,' which acknowledges the unique role of museums in society and their status as institutions of trust (NEMO, 2024). NEMO signals the need for museums to play an active role in the development of ethically informed practices related to the regulation of emerging technologies (NEMO, 2024). As custodians of cultural heritage, museums must pay attention to emerging technologies and how they are shaping cultural output and engage in governance and regulation activities to ensure their own roles are able to facilitate long-term custodianship and preservation. For example, a collective in the United Kingdom led by academics Oonagh Murphy and Elena Villaespesa has also been exploring the ethical implications of AI use in cultural organisations. To assist museums in dealing with the challenges, this collective developed 'AI: A Museum Planning Toolkit,' which offers case studies and informative worksheets (Murphy & Villaespesa, 2020). The aim of the toolkit is 'to support non-specialists to better understand the possibilities of these technologies, and empower a wide range of museum professionals to develop strategically, ethically, and operationally robust project plans' (Murphy & Villaespesa, 2020). While not specifically designed to address social media collecting, several of the core principles are applicable, in particular ensuring that 'human quality assurance processes [are] in place' (Murphy & Villaespesa, 2020). The Smithsonian likewise developed an AI values statement in 2020 to guide cultural heritage organisations seeking to make apparent any underlying biases and appropriately label content (Smithsonian, 2022). In particular, this involves museums critiquing data sets with which they engage to determine whether they have been ethically collected and that they do not perpetuate systemic racism and are not offensive. This value statement highlights museums' accountability for the methodologies, data sets, collections and algorithms they are using and the need to consider how they document these decisions. The Smithsonian statement recognises the challenges of provenance, especially in a postcolonial context, to confirm that objects were not acquired illegally or unethically. Furthermore, contemporary museological practice dictates that descendant communities must also provide consent and/or support for acquisitions of their own cultural heritage. This is particularly important for communities that have been oppressed by colonial practices. This logic extends to born-digital and social media objects, where museums must work with regulatory bodies and technology companies to determine who should be consulted and who needs to consent to acquisitions.

Conclusion

In this chapter, we have explored some of the current and emerging ethical challenges of social media that warrant consideration by museums. We have outlined the challenges of storage and its role in environmental sustainability to encourage museums to be more intentional about what and how to collect social media. Specifically, we have articulated that selective and representative – rather than comprehensive – collecting is an ethical practice that aligns with a museum's social responsibility. We addressed the amount of control that platforms have over creator content and the kinds of intervention or interference they have the right to make, which impacts the pace at which museums need to collect social media content. We also canvassed issues in the context of privacy and protection, noting that the publicness of social media content does not obviate the fact that those who donate or sell objects (physical or digital) to museums are individuals whose privacy requires protection. This is compounded by the Right to be Forgotten, which dictates that creators have the right to remove their content from the internet. Museums will be expected to pay closer attention to rights and permissions, and this may determine which collecting approach they adopt to ensure creators understand what it means for their content to enter a museum collection. We briefly articulated the complexity of who is involved in social media beyond creators – that is, the corporate players with commercial interests and how they can impact social media objects over time. Finally, we unpacked the rise of synthetic media and the complications it presents in determining authenticity, where museums might be compelled to move beyond the logics of physical objects towards a more complex understanding of authenticity that incorporates content created through AI and synthetic media.

While there are many more challenges in the world of social media that can impact museums, we have sampled those we believe curators need to be aware of in order to make decisions about collecting social media for their cultural collections. The challenges described highlight the complexities of collecting social media and the urgent need for research and practice to ensure that an important historical record of human experience is not lost because it is perceived as too complicated to collect. Nevertheless, we advocate for an approach to collecting in the online space that is informed by education and knowledge rather than risk. Our intention has been to acknowledge those risks but encourage movement through them in good faith. If museums can build flexible processes for collecting social media, including practices around deaccessioning, then we will be able to capture some of what might otherwise be lost.

Insights from practitioners

Suse Anderson

> It's easier for museums to be ethical in displaying social media collections if they also have protocols for how someone [and their content] can be removed really quickly and really easily.

Suse Anderson, Associate Professor of Museum Studies at George Washington University and former host of Museopunks – the podcast for the progressive museum – discussed the ethics of collecting social media with us. Suse's work focuses on the intersection of museums and technology. More recently, her work has been concerned with contemporary ethical dilemmas confronting the museum field.

Social media as cultural documentation

Suse explained that social media captures emotional, immediate and ephemeral responses to life moments and events, making it a vital form of contemporary cultural documentation. She highlighted that museums must now grapple with how to preserve and interpret what have become fleeting yet meaningful online expressions.

Disentangling collecting from display

Suse highlighted the requirement to distinguish between collecting and displaying social media. Not everything collected needs to be shown immediately. Some content will be both ethically challenging and traumatic, and extremely important to history and culture. Rather than not collect the challenging content because it might not have an immediate or short-term display, in her view, museums need to consider timing, context and risk when deciding how and when to display digital content. In doing so, opportunities to collect challenging content, especially in the social media space, might be seen as less of a risk.

Algorithms and diversity

Suse stressed the importance of diverse representation in social media collections and warned against the biases introduced by algorithms. We have all seen examples of white faces being preferred over Black faces by algorithms, and that doesn't even scratch the surface of algorithmic bias. Suse believes museums need to consider more collaborative models when collecting social media that include community curators – as active members of source communities affected by social media collecting – to ensure broader and more inclusive perspectives are captured in social media collections.

Protocols and the Right to Be Forgotten

Suse discussed the Right to Be Forgotten and advocated for museums to develop protocols that allow contributors to revoke consent and be forgotten if desired. This logic reflects the dynamic and personal nature of social media. It also replicates the logics of some social media platforms that delete all user data (supposedly) when a user deletes a profile and leaves a platform. In a museum context, this proposition aligns with ethical practices in trauma-informed collecting to which museums already subscribe.

Dragan Espenschied

> Instead of approaching the internet as a series of documents, it's more realistic to view it as a phone call. You pick up a phone and call someone and talk with

> them. You cannot really claim that you are representing a point in time but instead you might say this is what I encountered when I did the following.

Dragan Espenschied, Preservation Director at Rhizome, shared with us his work in digital preservation, which he describes as a form of 'resistance' in a space where things are 'constantly changing without notice.' Dragan stewards ArtBase, a collection of more than 2200 works of digital art and net art. He has a background in net activism, net art and electronic music. As a conservator, his work focuses on infrastructure, web archiving, emulation and linked open data.

Thoughtful collecting

Dragan explained that it is not always possible to follow the usual processes or practices when going about capturing content, 'or else you can't do anything' – this, he says, includes acquiring permissions in a social media environment. Instead, Dragan stresses the importance of doing things 'thoughtfully' and 'taking into account who might be harmed' as a result of collecting activity, then 'working closely with the communities you are collecting,' keeping in mind the importance of contextual privacy: Some people may be comfortable sharing content at one time in their life and may feel differently later on.

Access and display

At the beginning of the preservation process, Dragan explains, there is a need for professionals to consider how long they plan to provide access to the content and the means of that access, along with other concerns such as the searchability of the content. Alongside these considerations, Dragan stresses that display is inextricably linked with collecting social media and must be considered at the start of the process. He highlights the importance of understanding whether you need access to particular software from the time of collecting, so the object can be accessed and displayed in its original context into the future.

Worm's eye collecting

Collecting digital cultural heritage should be strategic and focused, rather than broad and comprehensive. Dragan refers to such an approach as 'worm's eye collecting' – that is, rather than a 'bird's eye,' which looks at a large field from above, worms tunnel down, focusing on a smaller field, and thus better understanding it. For example, a worm's-eye approach to collecting could involve using a user-driven web archiving tool to document social media. This archiving tool would allow you to visually represent the virtual environment of a social media object, the context in which it was created and published, and how other users engaged and responded to it. This approach makes it possible to better understand the object, both now and into the future.

Kirsty Cox

> Curators need to understand the financial ramifications of the storage and maintenance of these objects.

Kirsty Cox, manager of the Collections Information System at the Museum of New Zealand Te Papa Tongarewa, discussed her extensive experience in digital preservation and born-digital collecting, both at Te Papa and previously at the Alexander Turnbull Library. She emphasised the challenges and responsibilities of managing digital assets in museums, particularly the need for robust systems, clear acquisition policies and curator education.

Infrastructure

Museums often lack the infrastructure required to manage digital collections effectively. Many well-used collection management systems are not designed for digital preservation, leading to storage inefficiencies and risks, including loss. It is important for museums to understand whether they can actually and technically house social media content for the long term before undertaking to collect it.

Curatorial literacy

Curators, she says, require training in digital file formats, metadata and preservation practices. This will allow for more robust assessments of objects, not only from a content perspective but also from a materiality perspective. In the short term, early consultation with digital teams is essential to assess the feasibility and implications of acquisitions alongside significance assessments. Conversations lead to better collecting!

Redaction

Collecting social media raises complex issues around privacy, copyright and consent. Kirsty advocates for redaction as a useful tool to ensure privacy and ethical considerations are met when collecting social media content. With this in mind, museums will need to be prepared to consider and treat social media, and presumably other digital cultural heritage objects, in different ways to allow for redaction – something that is largely unconsidered when it comes to physical objects in museum collections.

What is worth preserving?

Kirsty explained that understanding the creator's intent – why they created the content and for what purpose – is crucial when making decisions about collecting and preservation. Through interviewing creators, museums can better make decisions about what aspects of digital objects are worth collecting and preserving and, most importantly, why.

References

Bode, L. (2021). Deepfaking Keanu: YouTube deepfakes, platform visual effects, and the complexity of reception. *Convergence: The International Journal of Research into New Media Technologies, 27*(4), 919–934. https://doi.org/10.1177/13548565211030454

Bode, L. (2022). From Holy Grail to deepfake: The evolving digital face on screen. In A. Maurice (Ed.), *Faces on screen* (pp. 288–302). Edinburgh University Press.

Casemajor, N. (2015). Digital materialisms: Frameworks for digital media studies. *Westminster Papers in Culture and Communication, 10*(1), 4–17. https://doi.org/10.16997/wpcc.209

Chan, S. (2022). Museum technology keynote: Words from ICOM 2022 Prague. *Medium*. Accessed 27 January 2023 from https://sebchan.medium.com/museums-and-technology-a-gentle-provocation-b9992c2e4455

Clegg, N. (2024). Labeling AI-generated images on Facebook, Instagram and Threads. *Meta*. Accessed 14 April 2024 from https://about.fb.com/news/2024/02/labeling-ai-generated-images-on-facebook-instagram-and-threads/#:~:text=We%20will%20begin%20labeling%20a,re%20uploading%20AI%2Dgenerated%20content

Crawford, K. (2021). *The atlas of AI: Power, politics, and the planetary costs of artificial intelligence*. Yale University Press.

deLuna, E. (2024). Gen Z mostly doesn't care if influencers are actual humans, new study shows. *Mashable*. Accessed 7 May 2024 from https://mashable.com/article/gen-z-ai-influencers

Edwards, J. L. (2019). An examination of consumers' social media trust in the wake of the Facebook and Cambridge Analytica scandal. In *CHI '20: Proceedings of the 2020 CHI Conference on Human Factors in Computing Systems*. https://doi.org/10.1145/3313831.3376662

European Parliament. (2024). Artificial Intelligence Act: MEPs adopt landmark law. European Parliament. Accessed 28 June 2025 from www.europarl.europa.eu/news/en/press-room/20240308IPR19015/artificial-intelligence-act-meps-adopt-landmark-law

French, R., & Smith, U. (2024). Deaccessioning: Why do museums remove objects from collections? Museums Victoria. Accessed 27 May 2024 from https://museumsvictoria.com.au/article/deaccessioning

General Data Protection Regulation. (2025). Everything you need to know about the 'Right to be Forgotten'. Accessed 29 June 2025 from https://gdpr.eu/right-to-be-forgotten

Gillespie, E., & Nicolas, J. (2024, 24 April). Queensland's state library launched an AI war veteran chatbot: Pranksters immediately tried to break it. *The Guardian*. Accessed 2 March 2025 from www.theguardian.com/australia-news/2024/apr/24/queensland-state-library-ai-war-veteran-chatbot-charlie

Glassman, D. (2020). Facebook is creating records: But who is managing them? *Archives and Manuscripts, 48*(1), 45–58. https://doi.org/10.1080/01576895.2019.1614077

Habgood-Coote, J. (2024, 13 March). Princess of Wales photo controversy shows we've been thinking about edited images the wrong way. *The Conversation*. Accessed 19 May 2024 from https://theconversation.com/princess-of-wales-photo-controversy-shows-weve-been-thinking-about-edited-images-the-wrong-way-225521

Human Rights Watch. (2023). Meta's broken promises. Accessed 2 March 2025 from www.hrw.org/report/2023/12/21/metas-broken-promises/systemic-censorship-palestine-content-instagram-and

Instagram. (2024a). Terms of use. Accessed 3 June 2024 from https://help.instagram.com/581066165581870

Instagram. (2024b). Delete your threads profile. Accessed 7 June 2024 from https://help.instagram.com/313703828012423

International Council of Museums. (2024). Museums storage around the world. Accessed 28 June 2025 from https://icom.museum/wp-content/uploads/2024/05/Report_ICOM-STORAGE_EN_Final.pdf

Jobin, A., Ienca, M., & Vayena, E. (2019). The global landscape of AI ethics guidelines. *Nature Machine Intelligence*, *1*(9), 389–399. https://doi.org/10.1038/s42256-019-0088-2

Kenderdine, S., & Sanderhoff, M. (2020). Conversation 5 Sarah Kenderdine + Merete Sanderhoff. In K. Winesmith, & S. Anderson (Eds.), *The digital future of museums: Conversations and provocations* (pp. 90–104). Routledge.

Kenderdine, S., & Yip, A. (2019). The proliferation of aura: Facsimiles, authenticity and digital objects. In K. Drotner, V. Dziekan, R. Parry, & K. C. Schrøder (Eds.), *The Routledge handbook of museums, media and communication* (pp. 274–289). Routledge.

Kidd, J. (2014). *Museums in the new mediascape*. Routledge.

Landsberg, A. (2004). *Prosthetic memory: The transformation of American remembrance in the age of mass culture*. Columbia University Press.

Lee, D. (2019, 10 May). Deepfake Salvador Dali takes selfie with museum visitors. *The Conversation*. Accessed 16 May 2024 from www.theverge.com/2019/5/10/18540953/salvador-dali-lives-deepfake-museum

Merritt, E. (2025). Stop, look, think: How to manage digital vulnerabilities. American Alliance of Museums. Accessed 28 June 2025 from www.aam-us.org/2025/01/20/stop-look-think-how-to-manage-digital-vulnerabilities

Meta. (2023). Introducing new AI experiences across our family of apps and devices. Accessed 10 February 2024 from https://about.fb.com/news/2023/09/introducing-ai-powered-assistants-characters-and-creative-tools

Meta. (2024). Privacy Centre. How long do we keep your information? Facebook. Accessed 2 March 2025 from www.facebook.com/privacy/policy?section_id=8-HowLongDoWe

Mihailova, M. (2021). To dally with Dalí: Deepfake (inter)faces in the art museum. *Convergence: The International Journal of Research into New Media Technologies*, *27*(4), 882–898. https://doi.org/10.1177/13548565211029401

Murphy, O., & Villaespesa, E. (2020). *AI: A museum planning toolkit*. Goldsmiths, University of London.

National Archives. (2023). *Digital services and carbon emissions in the heritage sector: Some preliminary findings*. Accessed 28 June 2025 from www.nationalarchives.gov.uk/archives-sector/digital-services-and-carbon-emissions-in-the-heritage-sector-some-preliminary-findings

NEMO. (2024). *Museums paving the way in an AI driven society*. Accessed 2 March 2025 from www.ne-mo.org/advocacy/our-advocacy-themes/museums-and-ai-conference

Rogers, R. (2024). TikTok's missing music is making users very upset. *Wired*. Accessed 14 May 2024 from www.wired.com/story/tiktok-no-sounds-taylor-swift-umg-licensing

Scott, J. (2024). Jason Scott interviewed by Caroline Wilson-Barnao and Craig Middleton, 26 March.

Smithsonian. (2022). AI values statement. Accessed 28 June 2025 from https://datascience.si.edu/ai-values-statement

Strauss, J. (2024, 3 May). Universal's music is returning to TikTok, ending a spat that hurt fans more than anyone. *The Conversation*. Accessed 14 May 2024 from https://theconversation.com/universals-music-is-returning-to-tiktok-ending-a-spat-that-hurt-fans-more-than-anyone-223324

TikTok. (2023). New labels for disclosing AI-generated content. Accessed 7 May 2024 from https://newsroom.tiktok.com/en-us/new-labels-for-disclosing-ai-generated-content
TikTok. (2024). Terms of service – limitation of liability. Accessed 5 June 2024 from www.tiktok.com/legal/page/row/terms-of-service/en
TikTok. (2025). Integrity and authenticity. Accessed 28 June 2025 from www.tiktok.com/community-guidelines/en/integrity-authenticity
Universal Music. (2024). An open letter to the artist and songwriter community: Why we must call time out on TikTok. Accessed 14 May 2024 from www.universalmusic.com/an-open-letter-to-the-artist-and-songwriter-community-why-we-must-call-time-out-on-tiktok
Vaccari, C., & Chadwick, A. (2020). Deepfakes and disinformation: Exploring the impact of synthetic political video on deception, uncertainty, and trust in news. *Social Media + Society*, *6*(1). https://doi.org/10.1177/2056305120903408
van der Sloot, B., & Wagensveld, Y. (2022). Deepfakes: Regulatory challenges for the synthetic society. *Computer Law & Security Review*, *46*, 105716. https://doi.org/10.1016/j.clsr.2022.105716
WeChat. (2025). Privacy policy. Accessed 29 June 2025 from www.wechat.com/en/privacy_policy.html
Zhang, Y., Liu, L., & Bi, C. Q. (2022). Influencer marketing and commercialization of social media influencer marketing and commercialization of social media platforms: How do consumers react to blurred-boundary advertisements? In *PACIS 2022 Proceedings*. https://aisel.aisnet.org/pacis2022/188

6 Conclusion

Collecting Social Media in Museums is underpinned by a challenge faced by the museum sector: That of collecting complex digital objects, such as social media. Beyond the technical challenges, a more concerning challenge for us is the variable and uneven recognition of social media as a valid form of cultural output and something worthy of museums' attention. This has resulted in a lack of action taken by museums to collect, with notable exceptions detailed in Chapter 4. In response, this book has argued for social media's inclusion in museum collections and has done so primarily from a curatorial perspective.

In Chapter 2, we acknowledged that social media is created in different everyday contexts, where it is embedded with meaning by creators who use it and understand it as a space to express their identity, maintain relationships and draw attention to the political and social issues that concern them, among many other things. This function of social media in society signals the importance of museums collecting it as a record of human experience. When it comes to museum practice, we have articulated how and why collecting social media differs from other types of collecting, including how it is unique from other kinds of born-digital collecting. We argued that collecting social media objects requires museums to adopt similar approaches to contemporary and rapid-response collecting by virtue of the ephemeral nature of social media and thus the need to collect quickly to mitigate the risk of loss.

In Chapter 3, against the backdrop of the sheer scale of content housed on social media platforms, we unpacked how museum professionals might go about determining what to collect and why – that is, how they might identify and understand the historical significance or otherwise. Furthermore, we investigated some of the new questions that social media asks of the practice of determining significance to museum collections, including the potential need to capture online environments, representing sociality and relationality, the role and influence of platforms, the intention of creators, contexts including human and non-human actors, display and interpretation, provenance and authenticity.

In Chapter 4, by researching and presenting different approaches to collecting social media used globally, we brought together examples and sometimes contrasting and contradicting advice about how to approach the task of

DOI: 10.4324/9781032669656-6

collecting social media in a museum context. This included automated archiving, donated content and data, collecting without collecting, collecting directly from social media, third-party service provision and simulation.

Within this complex collecting environment, there are, as we outlined in Chapter 5, a range of ethical issues and considerations that make collecting social media challenging at any given moment in time. Not least of these is that social media can be the home of hate speech, bigotry and bullying. Differing copyright contexts, the ever-changing policies of platforms, and varying global approaches to governance and regulation all make the task especially hard. As technological change, including the rise of synthetic media, is rapid and outruns legislation and policy at every step, there is no doubt that the museum sector will continue to be faced with such challenges well into the future.

Despite the challenges, we remain optimistic and continue to advocate for the need for museums to collect social media due to its many different and important uses and functions in our everyday lives. The social media we argue for museums to collect will help future generations understand people whose lives are currently enmeshed with social media use. In doing so, social media objects will serve to preserve social practices and traditions, to document moments of local and global crisis, and to understand the role of web-based and social technologies that have, and will continue to have, informed the identity work of individuals and communities around the world. Like physical artefacts collected by museums, social media objects help us to understand the past, make sense of the world around us and highlight social issues such as inequality and discrimination. They also serve to bring to the fore challenging topics and events that call for public scrutiny and attention, and help us to imagine our futures. Before we know it, technological change surpasses us, companies and corporations wind up, and social, cultural and political trends go in and out of fashion. Therefore, we argue that it is important to adopt a proactive mindset to collecting social media and to educate yourselves and your colleagues about how to understand, care for and handle these types of objects.

This book concludes in two sections. First, we put forward core principles that we hope will assist cultural professionals to advocate for and collect social media in a museum context; second, we summarise some of the key takeaways of this book, which we believe will support museum professionals in their collecting activities and warrant attention for future research.

Core principles

The following principles have been developed from what we have learnt through the creation of this book. This includes what we heard from the professionals we interviewed who all at various moments in their interviews talked about the need to experiment, to try different approaches and to 'give it a go.' Everyone with whom we talked acknowledged the importance of social media – from a range of perspectives – and the need for museums to pay attention. While their ideas and approaches varied, their sentiments about the work were often consistent. This, coupled with the scholarly research and case studies of those museums and other organisations that have been working in this space, has led us to establish the following core principles.

Acknowledge the importance of digital cultural heritage

Digital cultural heritage is important, even if we do not yet understand it all. Many people believe social media is frivolous, a low form of culture and a distraction. Yet when we pay attention to creators and their content, we can better understand how a whole generation of people have used social media to build their identities, to create communities and to do social good. This is not to discount the negative aspects of social media and internet cultures, which exist in parallel. By collecting social media, museums can better represent the accounts of everyday people in public life and attempt to document the lives and experiences of under-represented individuals and communities, thus creating a more robust historical record of, by and for society. Regardless of your experiences, even if you consider yourself a Luddite, hop on social media, explore and get to know a part of the world you never thought you would. It is true to say that many of the topics and themes that museum professionals explore are not part of their everyday lives – we don't expect curators of ancient Roman material culture to participate in gladiatorial pursuits – but that does not make them any less important. So, give social media the same respect as you would other forms of cultural experience and production.

Don't collect everything – be intentional rather than comprehensive

Social media objects are networked forms of communication that hold cultural and historical value. These objects (videos, photos, comments, filters, music and so on) actively inform collective memory and help to guide current and future understandings of the world. Given the breadth of objects housed on social media, it is important for collecting initiatives to be intentional in their approach, much like those associated with contemporary and rapid-response collecting. Because of this, the curator's role becomes even more important when collecting social media. As with the other objects that museums collect, practitioners need to prioritise social media artefacts that meet the individual collecting institution's mission statement and collecting policy and framework. We encourage those responsible for building cultural collections to identify a topic, theme or area relevant to their museum that manifests in some way on social media. Commit to collecting a small number of objects that represent that topic or theme, and experiment with how you might collect those objects. With intention, a social media collecting project can result in meaningful collections that are not only relevant to the mission of your museum but to your audiences, too.

Don't wait – engage now and be adaptable

Social media is not being archived systematically. Unlike government records, newspapers and other forms of legacy media, there are no regulations to keep or archive social media. Therefore, museums must recognise that loss is a fundamental aspect of the social media landscape. Loss can occur from inaction, technological obsolescence, corporations collapsing, creators deleting their own data and more. A rapid-response approach to collecting social media is required to mitigate the risk of loss. We encourage museums to treat social media as a research tool and a place where social media objects live. If museums don't engage in social media, they may never know what they are losing. Curators must pay attention to what is happening on social media, as relevant to their institution's mission. When something significant happens, or when a social media post speaks to a curatorial rationale, don't let it sit for too long; instead, act and work through how it might be captured and brought into your collection. It is all too easy to sit idle, wait for someone else to do it or think 'something else will come up.' This is not always the case, so museums and their professionals must be ready to engage with significant social media when it is identified.

Experiment frequently and widely

Social media objects challenge usual approaches to collecting in museums, which are deeply entrenched in the physical world. Because there are many different approaches to collecting social media, and this can vary based on the type of collecting institution and mission statement, if we rely on traditional methods of acquisition, we can risk inaction and loss of social media heritage. Laws and legislation might never catch up to museums' needs when it comes to collecting digital-born and social media objects, and best practices will continue to evolve as we experience technological advancement and change. Therefore, experimentation is key – try to try again. Collect one way, learn from it and try a different way next time. We encourage museums to start small and experiment with different approaches. Through this work, we believe the value of social media will be sufficient evidence. If we do not try, we will lose important historical content and data.

Seek consent, but within a risk-positive approach

Social media is of, by and for humans – people like us, like you, like your family and friends. Museums are custodians of objects and stories that reflect real people's lives. Therefore, ensure creators, users, players and actors who have contributed to any social media you intend to collect provide informed consent for museums to collect, in the same way museums seek consent for physical objects collected. Concerns about privacy online will continue to increase and be compounded by emerging legislation, including the Right to be Forgotten; consent therefore becomes more important when collecting social media.

Without such consent, museums risk breaching trust with their publics and compromising the human rights decisions of people who may choose to remove their digital footprint from public view. To avoid such reputational damage, museums must include creators in decisions about collecting and be upfront with the implications of donating social media content to museums. This is often the most challenging aspect of collecting digital-born material, and in articulating the importance of consent, we also want to encourage a risk-positive approach. In many cases – and this goes for physical objects too – consent can't always be granted at the time of acquisition, so more flexible ways of bringing objects into collections might need to be considered while rights and permissions are sought. We encourage museums to ensure that they work towards seeking consent while not letting the challenges hinder collecting, once a collection is acquired, it is only the beginning of its new life, and seeking consent should be considered one of the ongoing responsibilities of a museum, from acquisition to display over time.

Embrace change and redefine control

Social media objects are, and will continue to be, a complex object type. Social media objects are also distinct insofar as they may be subject to continual change as they continue to circulate online long after they have been collected by a museum. Museums must accept and embrace change and redefine their understanding of control as it relates to collections. Unlike physical objects collected by museums, which are taken out of their original contexts and placed into the museum storage and controlled in strict ways – including movement, decisions about their display and how they are interpreted – social media objects have different lived realities that require museums to shift their understanding of control and the role they have in the life of the object, which may be accessed by online users long after a version of it is collected by a museum. Alongside this, technological changes may require a change-positive approach. To keep fragile digital material for long periods of time and for the benefit of future generations, social media objects may require alteration – file types, storage solutions, display approaches and so on. We can learn a lot from time-based media conservation to assist us in the decisions we make through robust conversations with creators at the time of collection to better understand how museums can care for social media in the long term. We encourage museums to think expansively about social media objects: If you collect something now, it will be a copy of something that remains online (this is okay). Review the online post regularly and determine whether further parts of that object need to be collected or whether the version you collected stands strong in its intention. There is something beautiful in thinking that objects have continued lives in their original contexts while still being captured in museum collections.

These principles are necessarily broad. We believe they offer guideposts for museums and the professionals who work in them to frame their work, collecting policies and approaches to collecting social media. They can be used, altered and changed based on context and, we hope, used to support arguments for committing to the work of collecting social media in museums and then doing it.

The final section of this chapter seeks to summarise some of the key points made throughout this book that we believe will support museums in their undertaking of collecting social media.

The unique role of the museum

Museums are one part of an ecosystem of collecting institutions. Alongside libraries, archives and art galleries, they have a shared responsibility for collecting objects that reflect society and culture with a long-term aim of preserving the history of people and ideas. While these various institutions seem to be doing similar things, each has a unique role when it comes to collecting and preserving culture. Museums' approaches to collecting are more representative: With no intention to comprehensively collect, they often draw on objects and stories that communicate shared experiences and histories. This makes museums the perfect repositories for social media. With a large and growing corpus of information and content, museums have the capacity to collect representative social media that can communicate aspects of human experience and history to benefit future generations in providing an understanding of how people's lives have been changed because of it. Curation and the role of the curator become important to the practice of collecting social media; rather than focusing only on the technical process, curators are required to identify the significance of things and unpack meaning in objects for broad audiences.

Policies and practices

Social media deserves the same attention as other object types. While some museums dedicate curatorial roles to themes and topics, others dedicate curatorial roles to object types – from ceramics to fashion and textiles and large technology. There are increasing numbers of examples of digital curators being appointed and acknowledged for their unique and urgent role. Nevertheless, many museums still exclude digital content from their collecting policies and frameworks and continue to focus on physical and tangible collections. We urge museums to embed social media collecting into the policies and frameworks that guide their collecting practices. This will not only empower museum professionals to undertake collecting and museums to overcome technical challenges, but will also reinforce and educate publics about the significance of social media to human history and culture.

An education role

As we have already acknowledged throughout this book, people are not bringing their social media archives to museums and offering to donate them. People who are in the thick of social media use and experience do not necessarily understand what they produce as artefacts and archives worthy of keeping for posterity. Public education has always been an important role of museums, so the role of museums in communicating the social, cultural and historical value of social media should fall within their remit too. For us, this means museums should pay critical attention to how they are using their social media platforms, committing to collecting social media and drawing on their core business – display and interpretation – to communicate this to their public. We encourage museums to not only collect but also to talk about it and engage with their audiences about what, why, how and when to collect.

The relationship between museums and platforms

The governance of social media platforms is uneven and unclear, specifically as it relates to archiving content. We do not really know whether or for how long social media platforms are required to keep content and where that content is held. While we do believe there is a role for platforms to acknowledge that what is being produced on their intellectual property is socially, culturally and historically significant, and that there should be remits for such platforms regarding archiving – in the same way as newspapers and government agencies are expected to have them – we also know that current regulation is variable, and it is unlikely that museums will have an immediate influence on platforms, which are commercial and private. Therefore, there is a need for museums to change their practices and to collect social media, no matter how complex and complicated this process may seem.

Ethics

As we have discussed, there are many complex ethical challenges for museums to consider when collecting social media, from environmental impact to privacy and permissions, synthetic media and the meteoric rise of artificial intelligence. It is not a museum's role to solve all of these challenges, but rather to understand them in the context of collecting and to collect with ethics in mind. That involves being aware, talking and engaging in ethical conversations with colleagues, creators and platforms and documenting it all. Once collected, social media does not have to be frozen in time, and ethical issues and challenges can be worked through in an ongoing way by museums open to dialogue and change. Within the context of ethics, be confident, brave and open – collecting will be meaningful in that way.

Future research

This book has focused on a core role of museums: Collecting. We believe this is one of the most urgent issues for museums as it relates to social media. However, once collected, social media will enter a context in which it is expected to be displayed and interpreted by museums. While there is abundant literature on how museums use social media, it is largely focused on engagement, marketing and digital experiences. In the future, museums need to grapple with how to display social media objects in a meaningful way. This will have an impact on how they collect such objects and what infrastructure may be required in the long term. We look forward to research and practice evolving as museums commit to collecting social media.

Conclusion

Our hope is that museum professionals, students and researchers in the field of museum studies and social media studies – and indeed anyone interested in social media and museums – have found this book useful. By bringing together ideas and case studies in one place, we have provided a context for collecting social media in museums that will benefit those engaging with the topic. More work needs to be done, and we hope to see more and more museums experimenting with collecting social media – trying and testing, and probably making mistakes along the way, while ultimately enriching collections that will endure as evidence of humans and their worlds. So don't let the fear of complexity or error stop you from collecting social media. The magic of social media and how it has shaped our society are important to document, and it is a collective responsibility for us to do so.

Index